IMPROVE YOUR HOLIDAY PHOTOGRAPHY

by David & Shirley Kilpatrick

HOVE~FOUNTAIN BOOKS

IMPROVE YOUR HOLIDAY PHOTOGRAPHY

First Edition March 1988
By David & Shirley Kilpatrick
Edited and Produced for Hove~Fountain Books by
Icon Publications Limited using Apple Macintosh™ and
PageMaker 2.0™ computer typesetting and design
Printed in Great Britain by
Purnell Book Production Ltd

ISBN 0–86343–110–0

Published by HOVE FOUNTAIN BOOKS

45 The Broadway
Tolworth
Surrey KT6 7DW

34 Church Road
Hove
Sussex BN3 2JG

UK Trade Distribution by
Fountain Press Ltd
45 The Broadway
Tolworth
Surrey KT6 7DW

CONTENTS

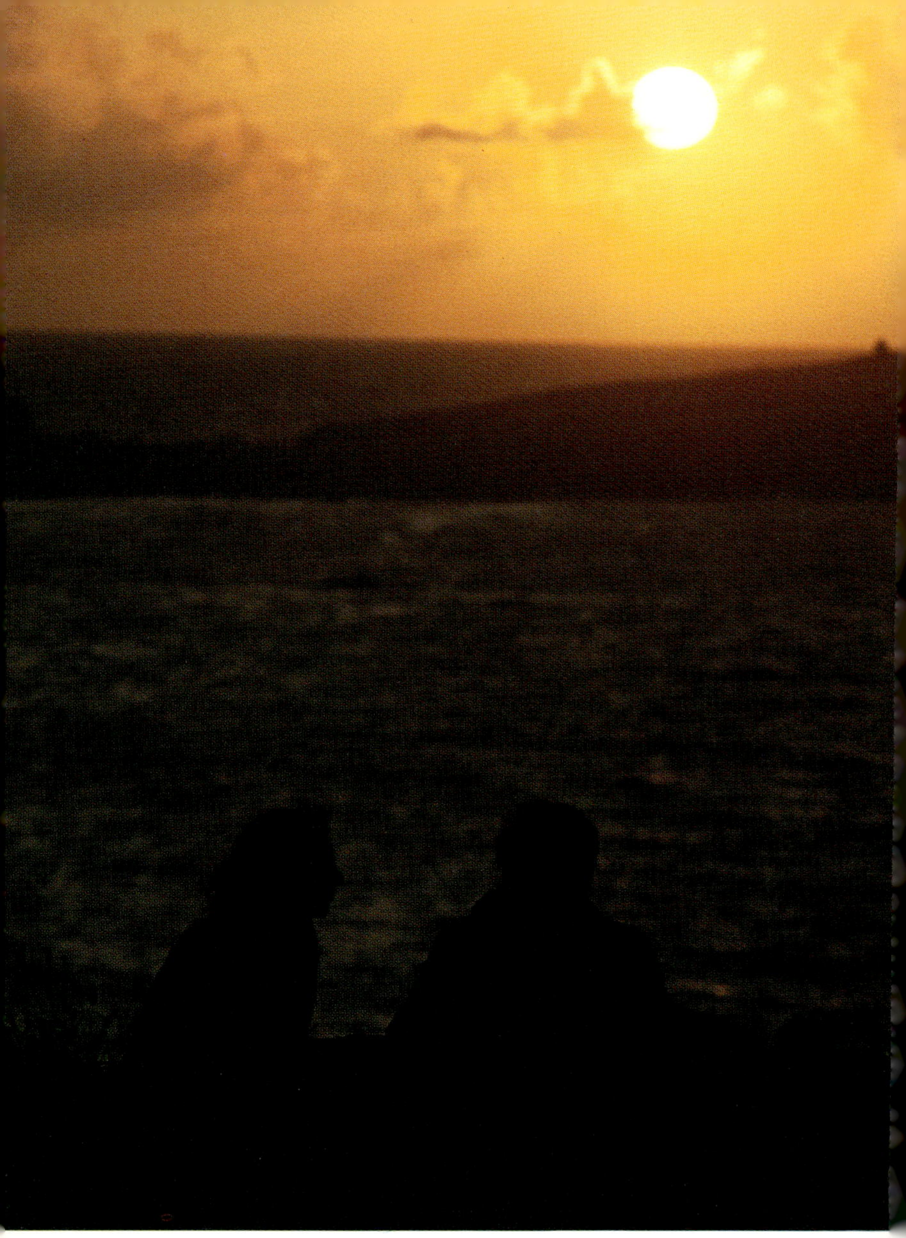

This book should be dedicated to everyone who ever watched the sun set into the sea... as well as the rest of us who photograph it

INTRODUCTION

EVERY holiday you take is a unique opportunity for photography – regardless of whether it's a weekend away, close to home, or a round-the-world trip. You are free from the worries of work and the daily timetable of office or home life; the places and faces are new to you, and if you are lucky the weather will be superb.

This book is here to help you bring back more than a plain record of your future holidays, to guide you in planning what equipment and materials to take, and to help you avoid some of the pitfalls. At the same time we hope it inspires you to use your holidays for better photography, which can be enjoyed by everyone.

Although we are professional photographers, nearly all of our pictures printed in books and magazines are taken on holiday, and not on exotic or uniquely photographic holidays! More often than not we book a simple package tour, take the children, and only use the kind of equipment which any amateur photographer might hope to take.

Once or twice a year we take groups of photographers on photo holidays – from beginners to experts – and every time round the results we see prove that even twenty people shooting the same subject take entirely different pictures. You, too, can take pictures which no-one has even taken before even at the most popular holiday destinations. Every sunset is a new one... but, as the REALLY keen holiday photographers will tell you, so is every *dawn!*

– David & Shirley Kilpatrick

1: TRAVELLING WITH YOUR CAMERA

MEMORIES of places you have visited and enjoyed are just as good a reason for your holidays as the chance to relax and see more of the world. For a good photographer, the memories are much more vivid and can be kept for a lifetime to share with other people. Many people never consider boarding a plane or even driving off for a weekend in the countryside without taking a camera.

For the non-photographer, the camera helps recall places, people and events. If you're a little more creative about your photography, holidays become ways of getting better pictures, and are arranged partly because the destination is good for photography.

If you think about the picture potential of your destination in this way, you should plan your photo outfit carefully. It can make a good deal of difference to the results.

Travelling light

Do you risk losing excellent pictures through travelling light and leaving half your camera kit behind? Many airlines stipulate that each passenger may carry only one camera, but say nothing about large bags full of equipment or awkward accessories like tripods. Refusal to accept a camera bag is rare and limited to low-budget or inland domestic flights in most cases. However, many camera outfit cases are available which are styled and sized to fit under airline seats, such as Zero Halliburton, Pelican and Andiamo. These expensive cases are rugged enough to withstand hold transit, securely lockable and will even float if dropped into the sea.

Practical packing

Few people want to go this far. Popular tripods pack comfortably into a large suitcase; lenses in padded or inflatable pouches can go in with your clothes as well. Carry one camera in a tailored pouch which fits to your belt and another, if you have two, in a small regular camera case with a lens and flash.

An approach like this means you are travelling light without leaving anything important behind. Many good soft camera outfit cases today have expandable sections, which zip up to create a more economically-sized bag when not full. Once at your destination, the extra section can be unzipped and filled with the equipment which you orginally had in your case or in other hand luggage.

Having this kind of case helps you on the spot. You may be going out for a short walk with the idea of stopping at a bar, perhaps staying out and eating; you know that the evening is the best time for lighting, and there may be a wonderful sunset, so the last thing you would do is leave

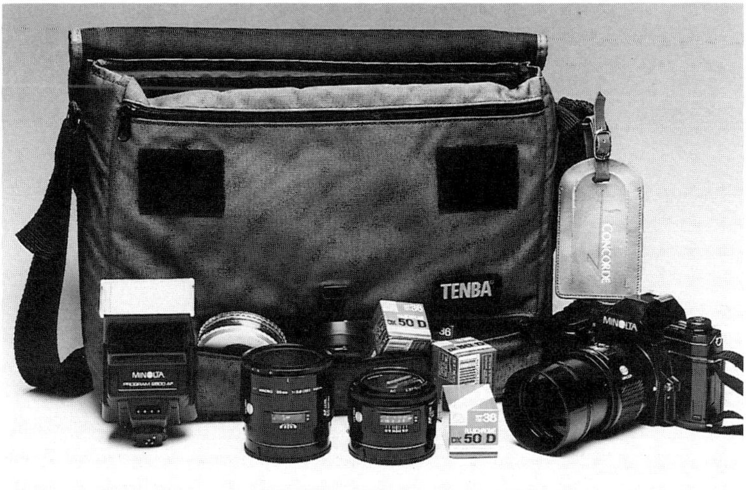

The best choice for travel outfits is often a 35mm SLR with three lenses and a few simple extras. A soft shoulder-bag like this one is slim enough to stow easily aboard aircraft – and doesn't attract thieves...

your camera behind. A soft bag with 'variable size' lets you take only the minimum kit you need, without being encumbered. On a major photographic expedition the next day you can fill it with everything.

Camera choice

The selection of a 35mm camera for travelling is not easy. The smallest, lightest and most automatic models are not the most versatile; the very latest SLRs with built-in film winders and autofocus are relatively bulky; traditionally reliable metal-built mechanical cameras are often big and heavy. The generation of small, light SLRs from the 1970s, started by the Olympus OM-1 and continued by the Pentax M series, is still around in the form of a few surviving models and many used cameras.

You probably don't pick your camera on this basis. If you have opted for an autofocus SLR, it will be fairly large and its lenses will be substantial as well. Zooms, which make ideal travelling companions, can be very heavy; 'outfit in one lens' zooms, like the **28-200mm**, are not convenient to carry around all day.

The minimum outfit should be an SLR with a **35-70mm** zoom

lens, a flashgun, and a pocket tripod or a pistol grip which clamps on to railings or the edge of a table, for night scenes and sunsets. Add to this a pocketable 'compact' **autofocus 35mm camera,** and you have a good start. Being more ambitious simply calls for a larger and costlier standard zoom; a **28-85mm**, **28–135mm** or even a **28-200mm** in place of the **35-70mm**, which is still the smallest and lightest zoom you can buy.

If you want to travel so light that an SLR is out of the question, consider a **dual lens** or **zoom lens autofocus compact**. This will do nearly as well as an SLR with a 35-70mm zoom, and better by far than a fixed lens compact.

A second SLR body, accepting interchangeable lenses, gives more versatility than the additional 35mm compact camera. Its standard 50mm lens is not a bad choice, because it is so light, even if the zoom already includes this focal length.

The serious photographer will prefer a separate wide-angle lens and telephoto zoom, possibly with the standard **50mm** left between the two to 'bridge the gap'. This is often a cheaper solution than a single **28-200mm**. The best all-round wide-angle at reasonable cost is the **28mm**; the choice of zoom is wide, but nearly all systems accept one with a range from **70 to 210mm**. Wide-angle zooms are more expensive, but one of these will allow you to replace a fixed **28mm** with a lens covering a range from, say, **24 to 35mm**.

A look inside a typical keen travel photographer's outfit bag revealed a wide-ranging system in only three lenses: a **24mm** wide angle, a **50mm** special 'macro' standard lens which allows close-ups of plants and insects at life size on the film, and a **75-300mm** tele zoom. These three lenses cost twice as much as a 28mm, an ordinary 50mm, and 70-210mm of the same make (but weighed about the same). For many photographers, the cheaper option would be just as successful on a normal trip.

Caring for your kit

On holiday you stay on the move so much that dust and dirt on your camera and lenses goes unnoticed. Apart from giving everything a good clean on returning home, you can do one or two things to keep equipment (and results) in good order.

First of all, do use a camera bag with a zip. The soft bags which only have loose flaps don't stop sand and dirt from entering. Secondly, buy basic accessories like protective lens filters, hoods, caps, ever-ready camera cases, lens pouches or cases, and cleaning cloths. Use separators or

Right: an autofocus camera lets you take shots of people quickly and unobtrusively

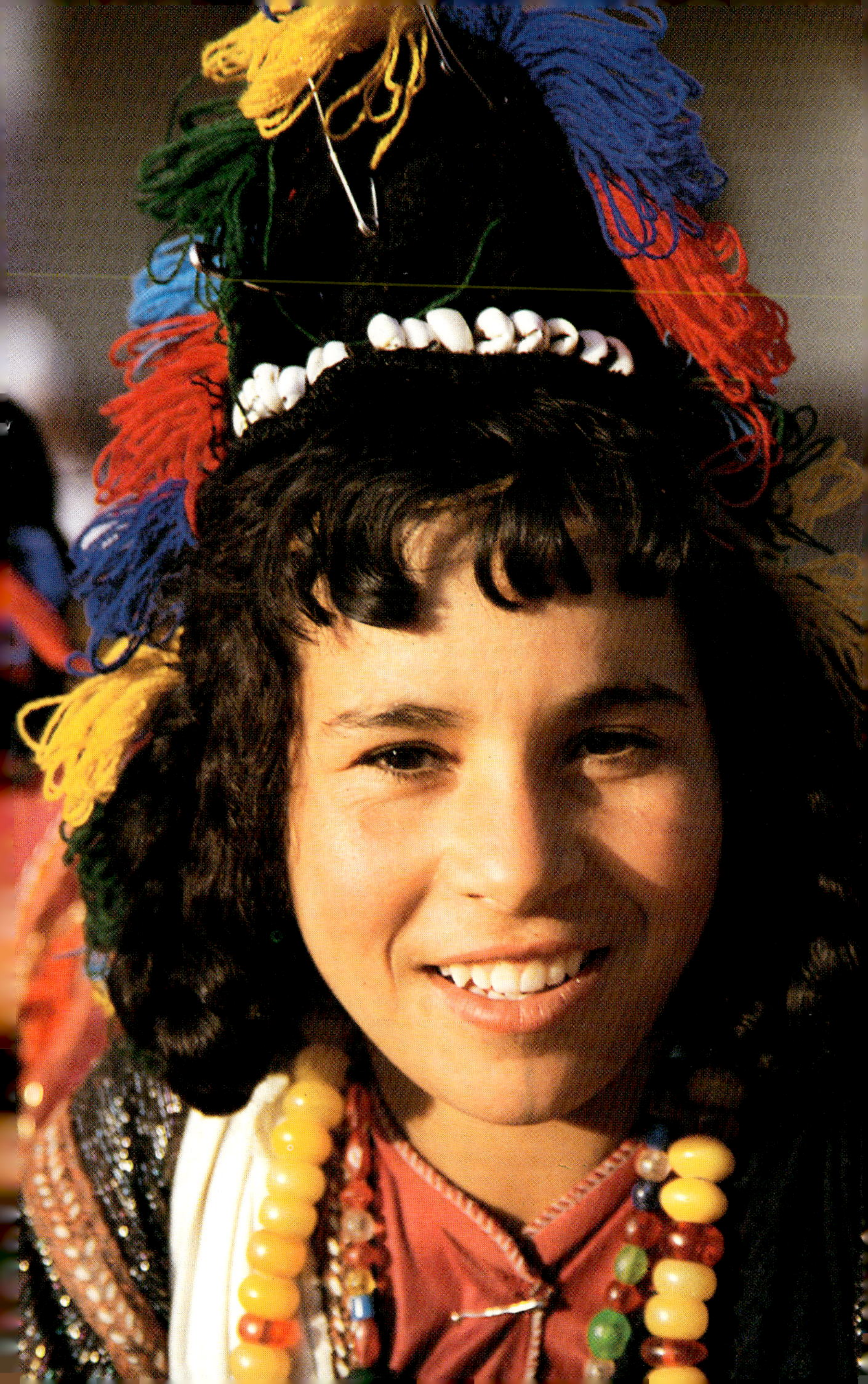

divisions in your camera case to keep items well apart, but where possible have lenses inside draw-string pouches as well.

A blower brush can be used to dislodge dust or sand. The type of soft cloth called **Selvyt**, intended for cleaning lenses, can be purchased in handkerchief-sized squares; keep a totally clean one for wiping filters or viewfinder eyepieces after breathing on them. After a few months this cloth can be used loose in the camera bag as a kind of extra padding or divider.

Avoid black cases in hot countries; left in the sun inside a black case, a camera can quickly rise in temperature to over 40°C. The same happens with black cameras if left unprotected. A reflective alloy case seems to be the answer to extreme conditions, if you are prepared to carry it everywhere. Remember, though, you will be marked out as a target by thieves.

Essential – or not?

Your favourite set of effects filters, complete with a large plastic holder, is probably not going to make or break your travel pictures in the same way it helps you along on a dull off-season day in familiar dull surroundings at home. Fisheye lenses, complete multi-head flash outfits, large tripods, bellows for capturing an insect's eye... well, unless you are an expert travelling with only insects in mind, or are putting photography first and everything else second, these things are best left at home.

A medium-sized **flashgun**, a **polarizing filter**, a pocket or lightweight **tripod**, a couple of **close-up lenses** or **extension tubes**, a cheap fisheye adaptor or a **teleconverter** – these things are a different matter. The simple close-up lens is a good example. It takes up virtually no space, but screws on to your zoom lens and allows you to focus on an object a few inches away. The telephoto converter takes up very little space and turns a **70-210mm** zoom into a **140-420mm**.

Batteries

Take spare batteries, particularly if you own a camera which uses a special size of lithium cell, triple-A 'mignon' 1.5v cells, or a meter cell such a PX-625 or G-13. Although you will find AA-size 'penlite' batteries of one quality or another throughout the world, you will certainly not find AAAs, silver oxide button cells or the even rarer lithium batteries in many small towns, even in the most civilized countries.

If you have rechargeable batteries, remember that the mains supply may prevent you from using your charger, and that they last only half as long as a set of ordinary alkaline batteries in any case. They are also more sensitive to cold conditions.

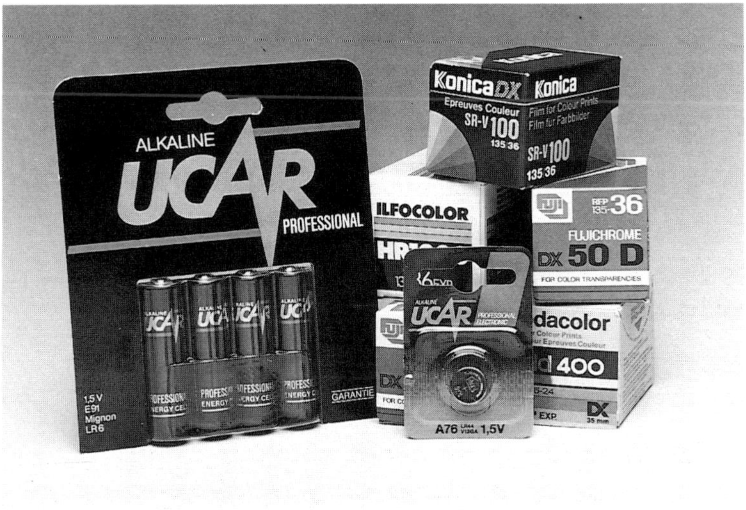

Buy film and batteries before you go

Film

Film always seems to be more expensive at the next destination! The best advice by far is that unless you have definite inside knowledge about cheap, fresh, branded film (Kodak, Fuji, Agfa, Ilford, or Konica) you should take all the film you need with you when you go. It is false economy to buy locally-made films in preference to the major international brands.

Film is best carried in a lead-lined filmshield bag, and left in unopened manufacturer's sealed packs of ten on the outward journey. Ask for a hand search at customs posts rather than the X-ray machine, but do so with a smile and hand over your film bag. Put your camera through the X-ray only if it is empty.

Do not object if individual film boxes are systematically opened, as this is customs procedure. Your lead-lined film shield bag will be useful throughout the trip to keep used and fresh films away from bright light.

Equipment and duty

The customs officers will only be interested in your equipment on your return if it is unusual or very new. In some countries you must obtain a proper form to record what you take IN to be certain of avoiding heavy penalties when you leave. Failure to do so may lead to confiscation of equipment which has a far higher value in a Third World or Eastern bloc state than you think; the duty charges 'owed' may exceed the new cost of the same items in the West.

It is usually enough to have a list of equipment and serial numbers and get it stamped on entry to the countries you are visiting. An insurance document listing values and serial numbers will do; so will a receipt for each item, or a list signed by a dealer confirming that the goods have been supplied, and when. Frankly, both the insurance and the list are precautions which anyone should take with any valuables taken on holiday.

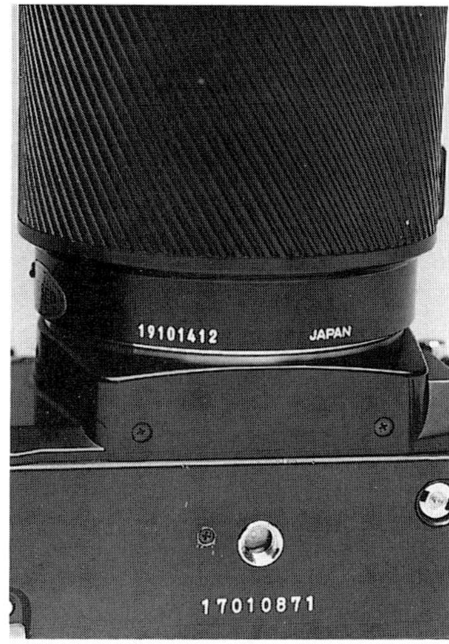

Most cameras have serial numbers which provide evidence for insurance and customs

Insurance

Most holiday tour insurance covers you for up to £250 of personal belongings – some deals offer much more. You must read the small print carefully. You will find that there is an single item limit, such as £50, and that your £500 camera is not covered by the £500 insurance. You would only receive £50. You might not receive anything whatsoever if the camera was stolen from a hire car or a hotel room; the terms require you to deposit all valuables in the hotel safe, and carry them on your person rather than leave them in your car.

Special photographic insurance normally costs around 2 – 3% of the total equipment value per year (say £10 for £500-worth) and will include replacement as new, agreed item values, full cover of each item, and up to 30 days total travel per year with exceptions such as mainland China. The travel terms can be extended by most companies by telephone, and sometimes there will not even be an extra charge. Your domestic insurance may well offer an extension – with or without extra cost – to cover travel if your cameras are included on this policy in a separate clause. If covered as general 'effects' the sum is normally too low to be adequate.

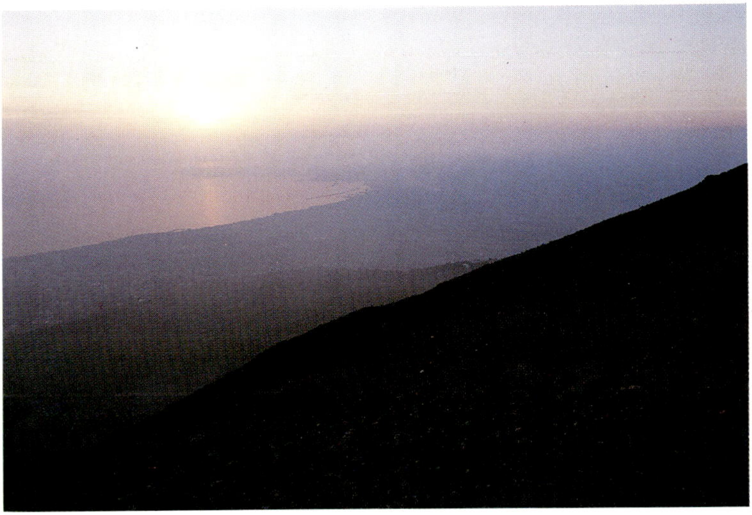

Holiday pictures can be unrepeatable. This subtle sunset from the rim of Vesuvius involved a hard drive and breathless scramble up the mountain path – with TWO cameras to take no risks

What if it goes wrong?

Right at the start, we looked at the idea of taking a second camera; if not an additional SLR for your outfit, then at least a pocketable 35mm compact. You will probably find this useful for switching between colour prints and slides, but you will find it infinitely more so if one camera goes wrong.

A darkroom enthusiast's changing bag is a useful item to take if you are on a long and serious photo trip. This zip-up bag allows you to use your hands inside a light-tight jacket, with the camera safely contained. Torn film sprockets, uncertainties about loading, accidentally fully rewound film, and so on, can be dealt with. You can use this bag in the same way as a lead-shield bag to keep film away from bright light.

Do not try to use overseas repair facilities. You are at the mercy of anonymity, postal delays, inefficiency or dishonesty. Keep your unusable camera until you return to base.

If you are tempted to buy a replacement, remember that an overpriced camera, heavily taxed in one country, is just as liable for import duty as a tax-free snip. Even secondhand cameras in some countries, like Japan, will cost far more than new ones in Europe – they too are liable to duty, and on the purchase price not the theoretical value back home.

Process in haste...

How about local processing? A one-hour minilab in Frankfurt may be better than a one week service in London (and you pay for it). Will the same type of one-hour minilab be as good in Delhi? Often the answer is yes, if you shoot colour negative film. Worldwide standards are now more than acceptable, with thousands of excellent developing and printing installations in the least expected places.

For the slide film user, the story is different. Standards vary greatly, even within the USA and Europe, and you get what you pay for. What is called a 'custom lab' in the States, a 'pro lab' in Britain and 'fachlabor' in Germany indicates a good standard of professional processing. The same colour slide film handed over the counter to a chemist or photo dealer may be tackled by a bulk photofinisher to rough-and-ready standards.

As for black and white, it is best to assume that most of the fun lies in processing the result back at home, so the question of local services is not relevant. You can, however, carry a 35mm developing tank very easily, and with the changing bag already mentioned and chemicals mixed from concentrates or powder you can see your results in your hotel room.

Be a good traveller

In someone else's country, try to respect local customs. Many people do not like being photographed (in any country) and they are not there as tourist attractions. It can help to carry a simple instant camera, to be able to give a free print to someone you particularly want to include in a shot. This is also where local developing and printing services come in handy. In some countries religious attitudes make photography impossible, and the travel guides for that area will nearly always tell you.

It is easy to assume that the natives are hostile or untrustworthy; this is rarely true. I have been led by the hand by Tunisian children, with great apprehension on my part, only to be shown their grandmother's house and orchard. When approached by an Indian asking questions about an old plastic Kodak film bag, I found he was a professional photographer willing to offer me a good leather shoulder-bag in exchange for it, so that he could clean it, stuff it with newspapers, and hang it up outside as an advertisement!

2: UNDERSTANDING YOUR CAMERAS

TODAY'S electronic cameras are not dependent on springs and precision mechanisms in the same way that familiar models from the past were. The mechanical parts of a camera are often electronically controlled – certainly as far as timing goes – and may well be purely electronic. With some cameras it becomes impossible to wind the film on, release the shutter or even adjust the lens aperture without a battery in place.

This has obvious implications for anyone travelling. The state of the battery is more important than the amount of film you take, particularly if the camera is powered by an inbuilt lithium cell. Some models have to be sent back to the maker's service agent roughly five years after their original purchase to have such a battery changed. Have you made a note of when this is likely to need doing if you own one?

Conditions

Mechanical cameras have always been affected by heat and cold. Serious travellers used to purchase 'tropical' field cameras with special hardwood bodies and treated leather bellows, and even now the best camera makers offer a 'winterization' service in which the lubricants are replaced with ones suitable for very cold weather and adjustments are made to tolerances and tensions.

Electronic cameras do not need such adjustments; they are normally made of plastics which can survive most temperature and humidity changes, have few mechanical parts, and use lubricant-free bearings. Their batteries are a different matter.

A pair of size AA (penlite) alkaline cells can be expected to run a compact 35mm autofocus camera for around 12 to 20 films in normal temperatures (20°C). At freezing point, the same batteries will power the camera for just three or four films.

A waterproof camera will put up with a good deal of abuse, but should you decide to change the batteries in the wrong conditions you risk installing a time-bomb inside the battery compartment. The corrosion caused by handling them in sea spray could damage the contacts or cause leakage. With conventional cameras using lithium or silver oxide button cells, you should not even touch the polished surface of the battery with bare fingers when inserting it – use a handkerchief or a lens tissue to handle the battery.

Electronic cameras, all told, probably travel better than mechanical ones. They are tougher, the plastic bodies resist impact without distortion or damage to the components inside, and there are fewer screws to vibrate loose. Without a battery, on the other hand, they are useless, and running repairs when travelling may be out of the question; a small craftsman repair shop can tackle a mechanical shutter, but not replace a central processor unit.

Electrical functions

FILM WIND-ON is now the most popular electrical function on ordinary cameras, even when these have simple fixed-focus lenses and exposure set for sunny days and little else. Normally there is no other means to wind film on when the motor is built-in; with SLRs taking a detachable winder, the manual lever-wind provides a second string in the event of failure.

Motorized film loading and rewind are equally important functions and go together with motor wind-on in many models. Automatic loading has the advantage that you can't put a film in your camera unless it is fitted with batteries. Auto rewind has the disadvantage that you can not recover or remove the film if the batteries go flat. One solution is a system which winds all the film OUT of the cassette at the time you load, and returns it frame by frame as you shoot; if anything goes wrong, you can open the camera back and remove the film manually, with all the shots you have taken safe inside the light-proof cassette.

SHUTTER operation is not always electrical, even when the exposure is automatic. Many cameras have mechanical shutters with a fixed speed (or two speeds) and a variable aperture controlled by the metering. It is just as likely, however, that the camera will have a fixed aperture and electronic shutter.

In complex cameras – including nearly all SLRs today – the shutter is electronically timed and operated even if it has fixed speeds, and all the exposure control is handled by changing the aperture.

A mechanical fail-safe speed is useful if you own only a single camera body. Not all SLRs have this feature, but it is common in professional models. The speed, which works even without batteries, is usually 1/90th to 1/125th of a second, and is suitable for flash pictures as well as general daytime shots. Some cameras also have a mechanical 'B' setting allowing time exposures.

METERING which relies on batteries more often than not forms part of an electronic shutter and aperture system, and is inseparable; if the metering doesn't work, the entire camera is probably dead. Separate metering is found on mechanical cameras, and does not affect the operation of the exposure controls even if linked to them via a viewfinder display. In the event of meter failure with a mechanical camera, you can always use a hand-held meter or the chart which comes with your film .

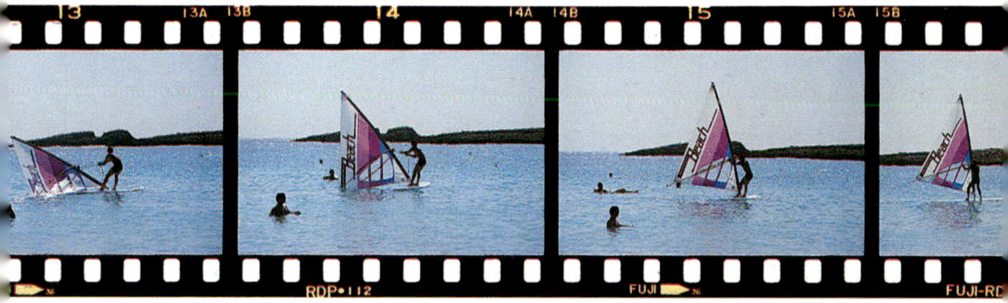

BATTERIES

Cameras with built-in motors are excellent for sequences (above) but may depend totally on fresh batteries for speed of operation. A set of four AA alkaline cells (left) will last most SLR cameras for around 12-20 24 exposure films, but if you visit an evening event where flash will be essential (right) always take a fresh set or spares with you.

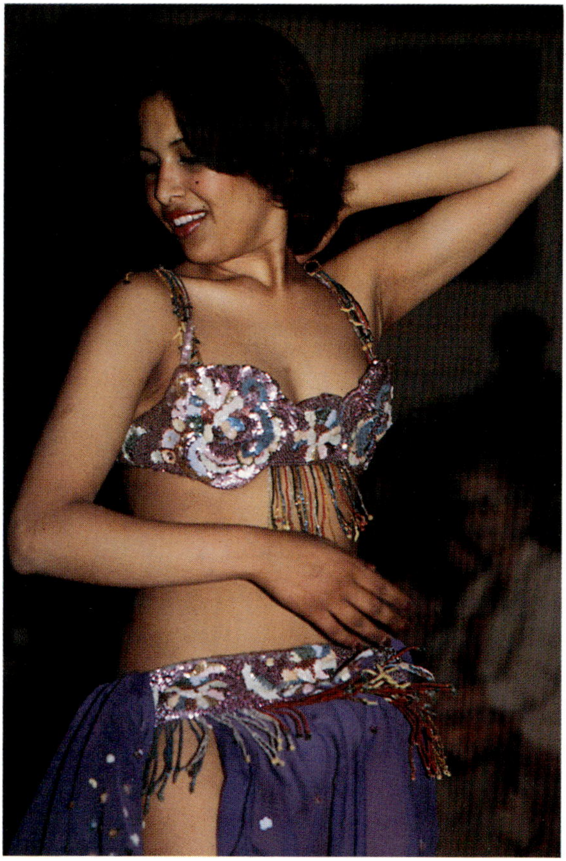

FOCUSING is only electrically controlled in autofocus cameras. As these cameras will cease to work entirely without batteries, you never need to worry about what happens if the focus stops operating. Most AF SLRs have the ability to be focused manually, which can be a help when batteries are running low and you want to conserve them.

FLASH UNITS have a considerable effect on battery life. Manufacturers quote figures for the number of rolls of film a set of batteries will last, based on 20% of all photographs being with flash. Sometimes far more than this are taken with flash, and the number of rolls can be halved.

When buying a compact 35mm camera for holidays, think whether or not you are likely to take many pictures in bars, after dark and so on. Take extra batteries! Watch out for those models which automatically switch the flash ON when it gets towards dusk. Instead of attractive sunsets, city lights or atmospheric shadows of a bodega you may end up with obligatory flash on every shot. Cameras like this, where the flash can never be switched off, are really intended for snapshot work.

A separate flashgun has many advantages. Firstly, it will be more powerful than the small unit built in or clipping to the top of your camera; secondly, it uses separate batteries and does not drain camera power; thirdly, you can choose when to use it. Many photographers too have been saved from battery failure by using the set in the flashgun when the camera's set unexpectedly failed.

Travel hazards

HEAT can damage cameras, batteries and film alike. The temperature of a camera, as we have already observed, rises sharply when left in the sun. To protect your camera when travelling, follow these tips:

* Keep your camera in its pouch or case

* Keep the cased camera in a soft fabric bag, light in colour, with plenty of space and padding

* Never leave the bag in the sun or in a car

* Complete outfits are best stored in foam-lined cases with a silver alloy or light fabric finish. Avoid black materials, plastics and cases without plenty of insulation

COLD causes most damage when you move in to a warm humid atmosphere out of the cold. Cold temperatures alone can do little harm to equipment, beyond rendering some plastics more brittle, lubricants sluggish and batteries weak. Condensation formed by bringing a cold camera into contact with warm humid air can do serious damage. If you see dew form on the exterior of

THE VALUE OF A GOOD OUTFIT CASE

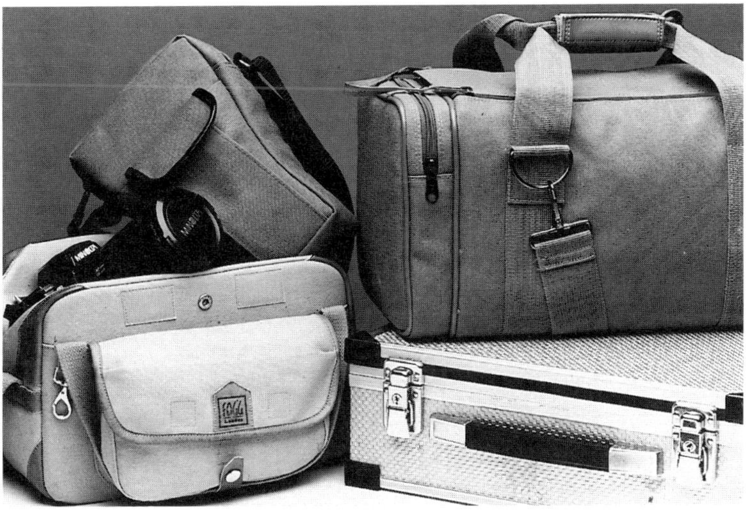

The best protection for any camera is a good case like any one of these types above, coupled with the use of a protective lens filter, lens caps, and the fitted ever-ready case for the camera itself.

the camera or see the optics mist over, DO NOT remove the lens or filter to wipe the surfaces; leave the camera with all caps, filters and accessories in place until it has warmed up gradually and thoroughly (allow at least 30 minutes).

After this has happened, you may load film or change lenses – but if you see condensation form inside the camera when you open the back or remove a lens, you must leave the camera open and wait again until the interior components have warmed up.

The worst situations for this problem are swimming pool enclosures, butterfly farms and tropical houses in zoos, or in tropical countries when leaving air-conditioned hotels, and coming inside to a heated area after winter sports.

VIBRATION can seriously damage equipment. The best protection is a well-padded case with a soft construction or foam liner. Follow a few rules:

* Never place a camera directly on the floor of a car, even if carpeted

* Avoid stowing cameras in aircraft holds

* Do not rest the camera against vibrating surfaces in boats, light aircraft or buses

DUST AND SAND...

DUST is not kept out by ever-ready cases or soft bags unless they have a zip. Flap closures are the most convenient form of bag, but zips are much better for holiday outfits; they are dust-proof and harder to steal from! The best dust protection is a gasket-rimmed hard case.

We keep our cameras in flap-lid cases, with very little dust proofing, but wrap each body or lens in a handkerchief-sized soft cloth. Every lens has a plain UV (clear) filter fitted, and the lenscaps are always kept on. After shooting in a dusty area, the camera is brushed with a blower-brush to remove the particles. At the end of a holiday trip it is carefully cleaned with a brush, soft cloth and cotton buds.

SAND is a worse enemy than dust and must be kept away from all mechanisms. To clean a camera which has been covered in sand will involve a strip-down. Do not try to operate ANY controls: even turning a focusing ring or winding the film on may permanently damage the mechanisms.

RAIN is naturally inimical to electronic cameras! The best advice is keep the camera dry at all times. Glass lens elements may be marked permanently by rain drops, and pictures taken when droplets are present will show small blurred patches. If you must shoot in the rain, keep an ever-ready case on your camera, use a polythene bag to shield it, get a friend to hold an umbrella, and use a deep lenshood if possible.

SEA WATER is worse than rain and the only advice is to ensure that sea spray and water never come into contact with your camera unless it a special weatherproof model. If they do, wipe off the moisture with a soft cloth immediately and clean any glass elements with a proprietary lens cleaner solution and tissue. If a camera is dropped in the sea, immersion in fresh water will do more good than harm though in fact you might just as well write it off for good; any repair will exceed the value of the camera itself, unless it is a Leica or Hasselblad...

SUNTAN OIL and similar greasy liquids will do very little harm to camera bodies or mechanisms if they have simply rubbed off by contact. But spillage on to a camera will probably ruin it permanently. Apart from the cosmetic disfigurement of matt finishes rendered shiny by oil, thin films do no harm. Getting oily fingermarks on lens surfaces is another matter; no long-term damage will result but your pictures will be seriously degraded and soft until you clean the lens carefully, using a lens cleaner and tissue. Removing sand and suntan oil mixed is a professional service job.

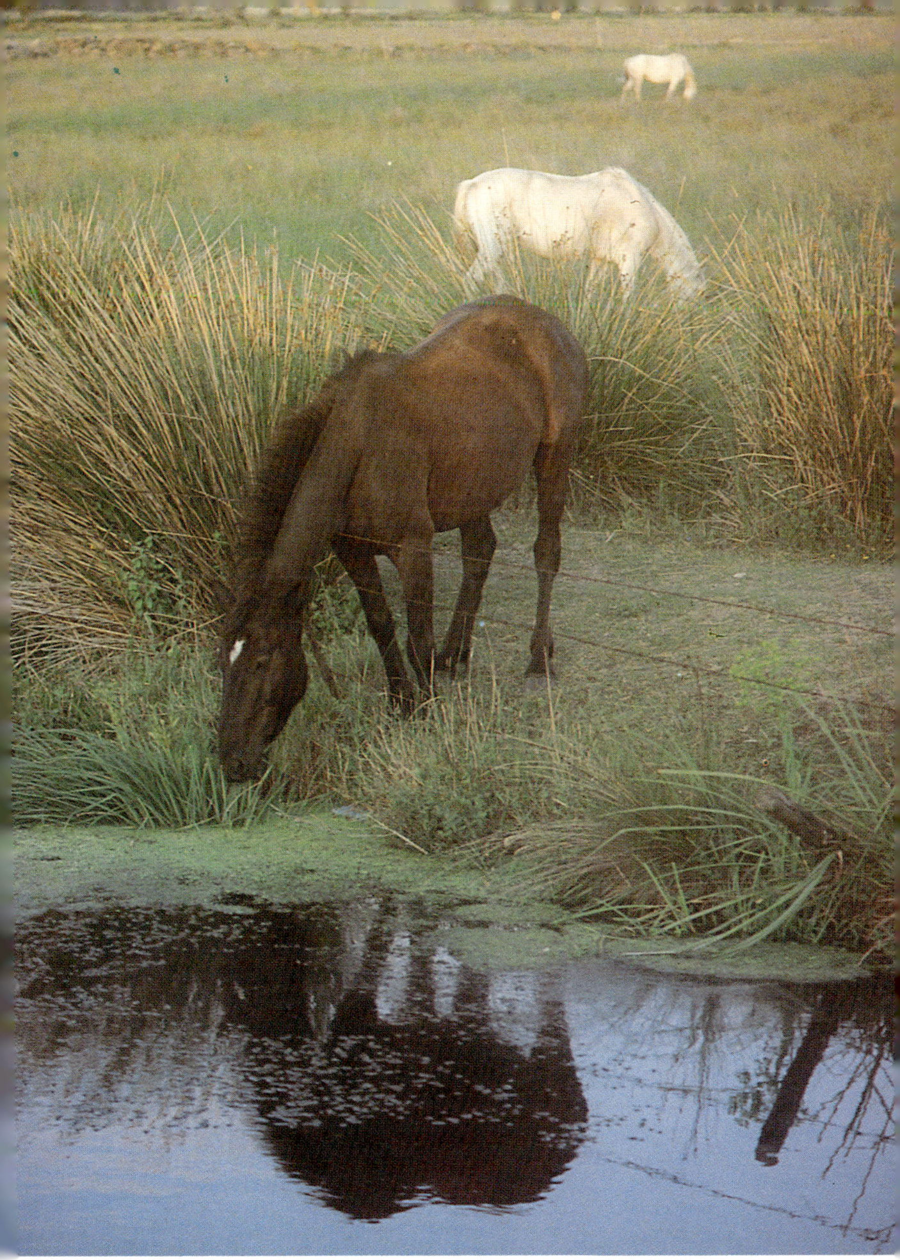

This is a misty and atmospheric picture, but it was a mistake! Soft focus suits horses in the French Camargue. It was caused by suntan oil handprinted on the front element of an Olympus 75-150mm zoom.

Exposure Metering

Exposure meters in all modern cameras are set to the same calibration based on an 'average' scene. The camera expects most pictures to consist of a fairly even mixture of dark and light tones, ground and sky, and this is assumed to be equal to a shade of grey which reflects all colours equally, absorbing about four-fifths of the light and reflecting back one fifth.

The actual figure used is 18% reflectance, which is rather like grey flannel suiting. If the scene in front of the camera does not average out to this blend, the metering system will make the wrong assumptions. Fill the frame with a white tuxedo suit, and the picture will come out as grey flannel... fill the frame with a charcoal pinstripe and sure enough, you get grey flannel.

This is the main reason why so many holiday shots feature mid-brown sand and dark grey sea, glowering clouds, grey white-washed houses and impenetrably dark suntans. Holidays tend to be taken in light, bright surroundings; beach, snow, water, dusty and sunny towns, white hotels, and so on. Holidays in green countries, in spring and autumn, produce much better pictures.

Practical tips

The first basic advice is purely practical; if you shoot colour negative film, set the camera's ISO (ASA) filmspeed control to HALF the value shown on the film box (if you are able to do so). No harm can ever result from this with negative film, and the chances are that you will greatly improve your results. It makes considerable sense to buy ISO 200 film and set the camera to ISO 100 for all beach, water and winter-sports holidays.

If you use slide film, or prefer to make full use of your film's speed for low-light shooting in the evening, you need a camera with a backlight control or an over-ride. The backlight control is normally a button which increases the exposure to compensate for the sun shining towards the lens and fooling the meter. You can use the same control whenever you are photographing on the beach, or in generally light surroundings, whether the sun is out or not and regardless of its angle.

Cameras with an over-ride control (a dial typically marked with figures from 0 to ±2) can be set to +1 when in these conditions, though with slide film it is always better to take two or three pictures – normal, +1/2 and +1 are suitable settings to try.

It is a mistake to buy a fast film (ISO 400) on the basis that setting +1 will reduce it to a 200-speed film. You are not actually changing the film's speed, just correcting for an error in the way the exposure meter works. Use

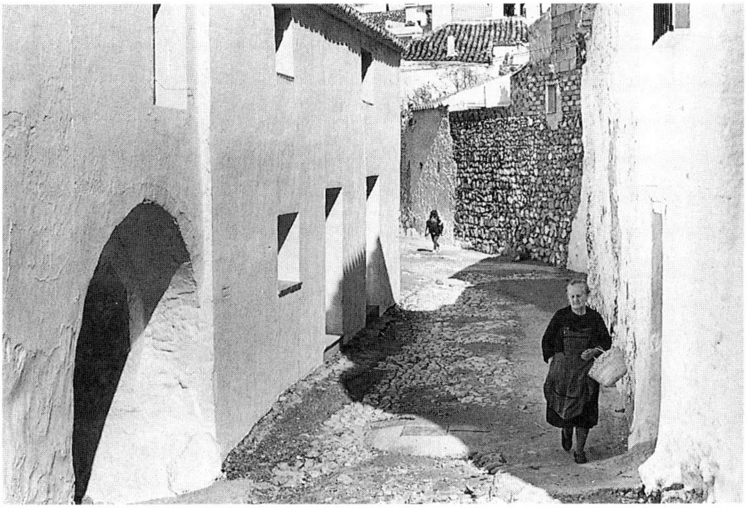

The whitewashed houses of a Spanish village need one stop more exposure than the camera meter indicates to record their true brightness. An unadjusted print would be grey in comparison.

slow or medium-speed films, in the range ISO 25 to ISO 200, whenever possible for holiday photography. Black-and-white users are probably knowledgable enough to need little of this advice, but a good tip is to rate your film at its normal ISO speed and then process in a speed-increasing developer like Aculux which adds 1/3rd of a stop (ISO 125 becomes ISO 160).

Metering to correct

If you are more advanced as a photographer, you can use the spot metering facility on many SLRs to zoom in on a medium tone such as a good suntanned face or a patch of grass, lock the reading from this into the camera's memory, and expose after re-composing the shot. Some cameras have metering which is capable of recognizing difficult lighting situations without the need for a selective reading.

More about focusing

Focusing is easy or automatic with most cameras now, but you should be aware of a few limitations. Cameras marked 'Focus Free' are actually fixed in focus – they are permanently set to about 2-3 metres distance.

FOCUSING PROBLEMS

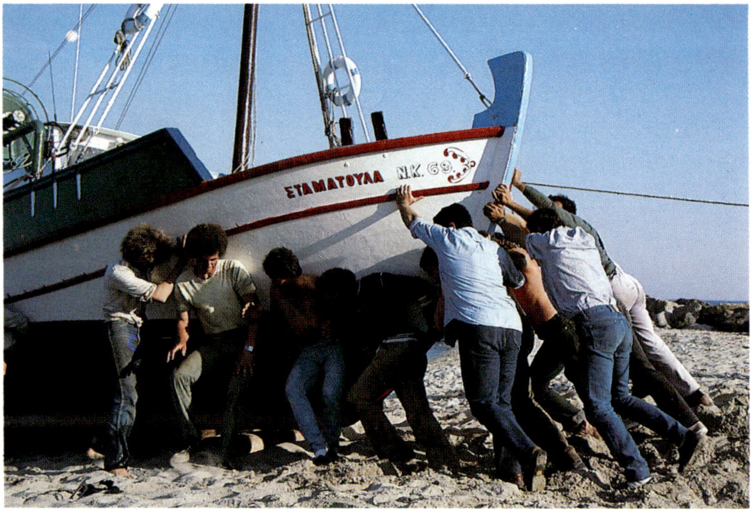

A simple compact AF 35mm camera keeps everything sharp in this beach scene without requiring great care in focusing. The 35mm focal length lens gives a semi wide-angle view.

Do not try to take close-ups with these. Even proper AF compact cameras have a close distance limit of around 1 metre unless there is special close-up setting.

Manual focus, where you must set on a scale the distance you judge to be correct, is reliable on pocketable cameras like the Minox 35; errors of a foot or so at normal distances have little effect. After all, similar cameras marked with symbols for 'zone focusing' on portraits, groups and landscapes work perfectly well most of the time.

Rangefinder cameras are uncommon now. They have a small spot in an optical viewfinder which indicates by converging images when a part of the view is correctly focused. They are very accurate, but the range of distances is no greater than an ordinary AF camera, from infinity to around one metre.

Single-lens reflex viewing, focusing through the lens, is the most accurate and versatile method whether auto or manual. With this system you can take excellent close-ups, but the cameras are naturally expensive.

All the pocketable, one-piece compact 35mm cameras are specially designed so that errors in focusing are unimportant. Even when you focus on an exact

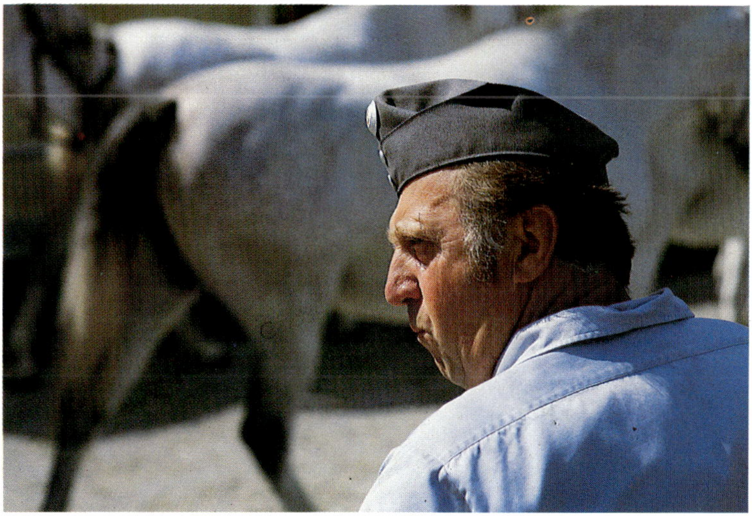

This Austrian official, in charge of Lippizaner horses, is picked out in sharp focus against slightly blurred horse shapes by using a 70-210mm zoom set to 210mm.

distance, like 2.3 metres, the depth of 'field' with sharp focusing extends from under 2m to over 3 in most light conditions.

This is not so with the kind of zoom lenses you will probably buy for your SLR system, or at very close distances like 30cm which most SLRs allow you to focus on. To ensure adequate depth of field, you must use a small lens aperture like *f*16 and probably put the camera on a tripod to use a matching slow shutter speed like 1/8th of a second.

Exposure programs in most cameras do NOT do this for you; they assume that depth of field is less important than preventing blur due to camera movement, and very often your zoom lens will be set by the exposure program so that your sharpness extends only a few inches in front of and behind your point of focus.

It is important to understand this when considering cameras for holiday shots. Unless you are prepared to work fairly hard at understanding photography, choosing your angles and viewpoints, picking your point of focus and perhaps even taking accessories like tripods, an SLR system may produce less satisfactory results than a simple pocketable camera.

3: PEOPLE IN THE PICTURE

HOWEVER well you remember your holidays for a year or two, you have no guarantee that the memory will last. If you have children or elderly relatives with you on holiday, you can be sure that their memories will be even more impermanent. You can probably remember your own childhood holidays, but how much of that recollection has come from seeing pictures of yourself later on?

For other people, photographs of your friends and family in exotic or interesting places can be amusing – particularly to those included in the shots. The secret of interesting 'self portraits' on holiday is variety, and you can't take too many, just as long as you never take the same background or group twice.

Let's say you are walking down the Champs Elysées. At one end, there is the Arc de Triomphe, a substantial and recognizable background. There is no point in lining up each of your party in turn in front of this. Walk away from the Arc, and a little further on you might find Renault's motor museum. This would make a good background for anyone (man or boy!) who loves cars. Later you might stop at one of the fashionable cafés – there you could photograph someone being served with wine or coffee.

When you pass the prints round, you don't end up saying "And there's Fred in front of the Louvre... here he is at Notre Dame..." repetitively. The only sin worse than this is a string of names in front of the same subject! Instead, your deliberate decision to photograph a different member of your group in each different setting makes the set of prints very interesting for almost anyone to look at.

Scale and composition

If you use a compact camera, the lens has an ideal angle of view for including people in general scenes at a reasonable distance. You have to think practically. Most popular landmarks, the instantly-recognizable backgrounds you want for your pictures, are busy. Crowds get in the way. If you try to place your subject more than fifteen feet from the camera, photography will be difficult.

With a standard 50mm lens, this distance means a reasonably dominant full-length figure will appear in front of a selective background. For the best shot, move a good distance away from large subjects. Take your picture of the Eiffel Tower from a distance which 'gets it all in' with the 50mm – that is ten minutes' walk away.

The 35mm lens of a compact camera, or the 28mm wide-angle on an SLR, are much better choices. You can get away with the subject as close as ten or even eight feet. At the same time, you can be twice as close to the background. If you want to shoot a person sitting at a café table you really need a wide-angle to include any meaningful background. In a railway carriage or coach, a passenger sitting in an aisle seat can lean back and take a good shot of the scene outside including a fellow-passenger in the window seat.

If the picture is meant to show the person and not the scene, the figure should be at least one-third of the height of the shot. The composition will be better if the person is cut off below the waist, so that space is not wasted on legs, feet and an expanse of ground.

If you intend to show the scene, and simply want to include someone for scale or to add a compositional highlight, make sure that your subject is NOT looking at the camera and standing in an 'I'm being photographed' manner. Have them pose naturally in an appropriate part of the scene, side-on to the camera, looking into the view.

In both cases, you should focus on the person, not the scene. Why? Because when the figure is large enough to be the main subject, this is where you want the sharpest focus; when the figure is small enough to be part of the scene, they will be at just the right distance for the best distribution of focus from middle-distance to infinity.

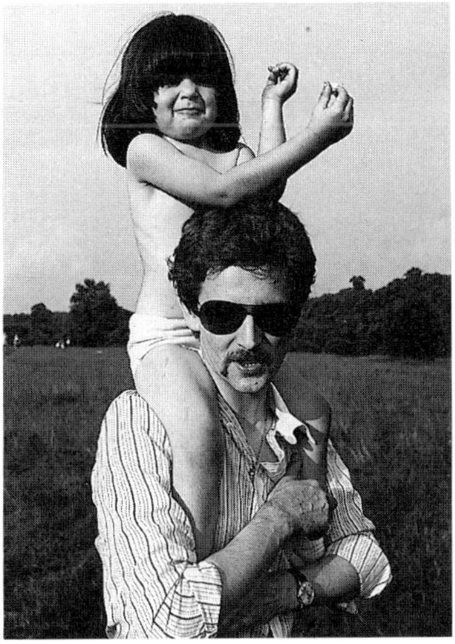

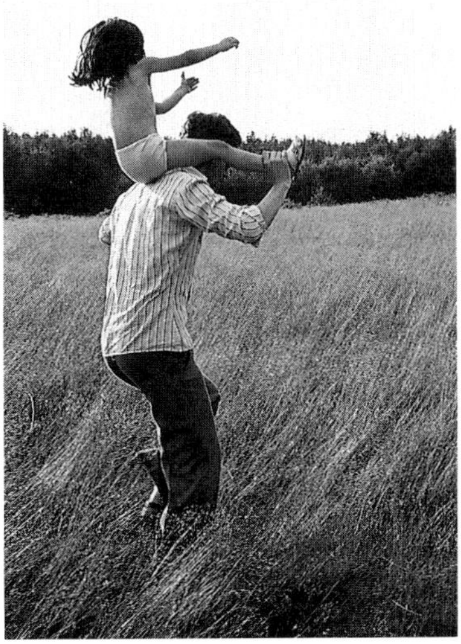

Top: the conscious approach. Bottom: a figure in a scene. In both cases focus on the figure.

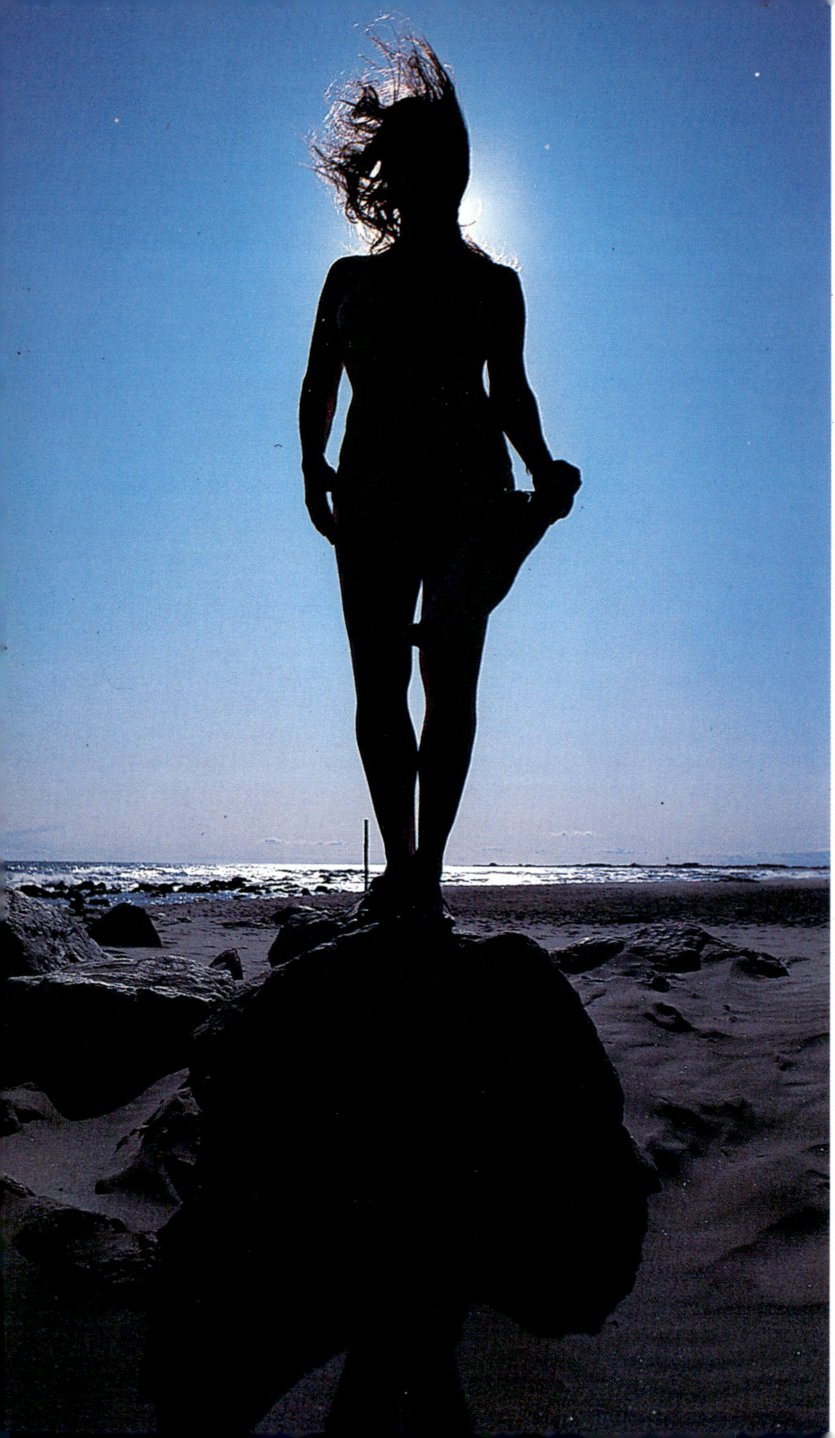

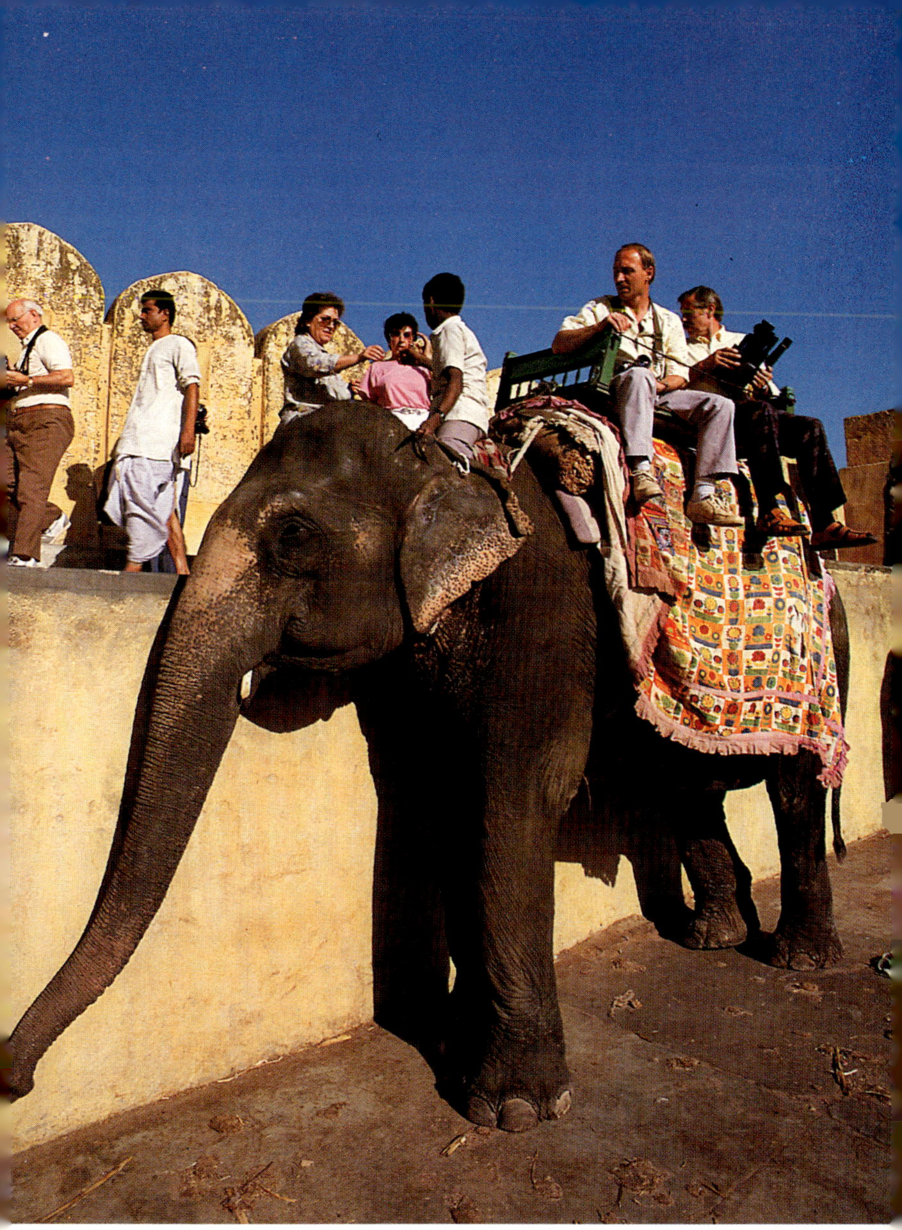

Left: a posed picture can work well if you aim for a dramatic composition and lighting – it's more than a holiday snap.
Above: an elephant ride makes a first-rate photo opportunity of a more conventional kind

As for composition, avoid putting anyone right in the middle of the picture. Follow the old rule of thirds – position your subject one-third in from one side, or even better, keep your person well inside that third of the picture, leaving two-thirds of the shot unimpeded. It can help identify vague places, like cafés or street scenes, if you include a sign in the picture – legibly but not prominently.

The self-timer

Most cameras are fitted with a device called a self-timer or delayed action. It has two main uses. The principal use for serious photographers is to release the shutter with a minimum of vibration when the camera is on a tripod. The traditional holiday use is to get yourself in the picture.

The self-timer symbol is normally marked on electronic cameras with **'ST'**, or like this:

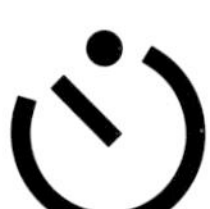

Mechanical models have a small lever:

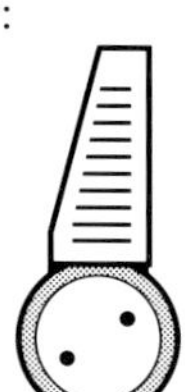

All self-timers are simply operated before releasing the shutter. A ten-second delay is normally provided, with an audible bleep and/or a flashing red light warning you that the timer is in action. Just before the camera is due to fire, the bleeping or flashing speeds up, giving anyone in the shot a chance to look at the lens and smile.

To use the self-timer properly you need a tripod. Compose the picture with someone else in the position where you want to be, or leave a space in a group. Never add yourself to the END of a group or BEHIND it, as you cannot be sure you will be included in the shot!

With SLR cameras, remember that having the sun shining from behind the camera can cause exposure errors unless the viewfinder eyepiece is capped. Your own eye normally prevents bright light from influencing the exposure meter system. Many SLRs have a shutter device to blank off the eyepiece; others come with a small plastic cap you keep attached to the camera strap.

Be careful, when composing a tripod-mounted shot, to pick a place where unsuspecting passers-by are unlikely to walk in front at the wrong moment. Keep the amount of sky in the shot to a minimum to ensure good exposure, and tighten the tripod's head up correctly so that the camera does not move.

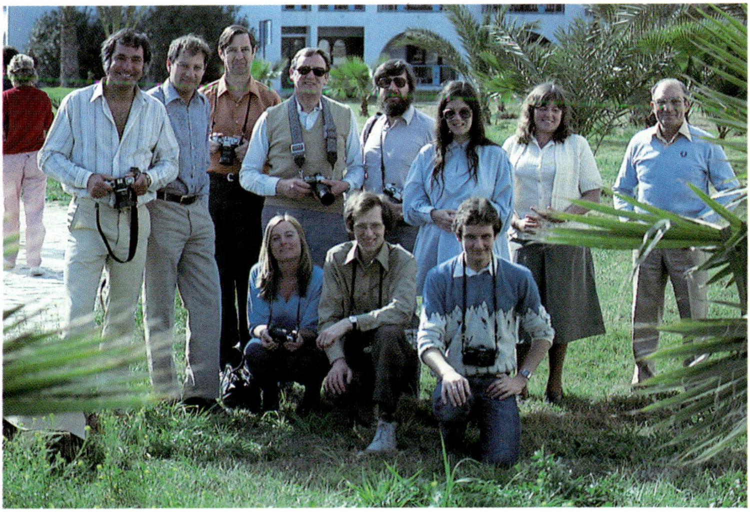

When you use a self-timer, leave a space in the middle of a group rather than join it at one end. A kneeling position in the front is particularly quick to reach after releasing the timer.

Local assistance

You know your camera better than anyone else. This will not stop tourist guides, hoteliers, waiters and all kinds of people from offering to take your picture. If you trust them with the camera, let them. It's a friendly thing to do. When we are abroad and see a group of people giving each other the camera and arranging permutations of a group, we nearly always offer to take one for them with everyone included.

Think twice if your camera is very valuable, not because of the risk of theft, but because of potential embarrassment if your 'photographic assistant' should accidentally drop the camera. Put the strap round his or her neck yourself. Doing this helps emphasize the value of the camera.

Don't allow anyone offering to take your picture to take more then one or two shots, and watch out for obvious tricks. There are plenty of helping hands around who will suggest that they can get your film developed and try to sell you a replacement, especially in Far Eastern countries. It is always far safer to ask a friend or someone you know to be another tourist to use your camera for you.

Suntanned and untanned

One problem you may encounter in group photographs with friends you meet on holiday is the different depths of suntan. Some faces go a bright red before turning a pleasant shade of brown and others may be totally white. Think about this when setting up your picture – if anyone is going to be in a shaded area, let it be an un-tanned person rather than someone with a strong tan. Ask anyone with a very white face to wear a sun-hat with a brim – this can be enough to make the picture look natural.

In general, tanned faces come out too dark against brightly lit beach and street scenes. Don't pose people against white walls in sunshine; even if they are fully sunlit as well, the contrast will be too high. Take your shots in open shade against mid-toned backgrounds. To emphasize a suntan put the subject against blue or green rather than warm colours. This is a trick widely used in holiday brochures.

Wet skin photographs darker than dry skin. There are many reasons for this, and if you want to produce an exotic-looking glamour shot a deep tan with oil and splashed water produces just the right result. Only use a polarizer if you want rich, deep skin colour. This looks appealing in carefully-designed calendar shots which are almost abstract, but wreaks havoc with faces.

Flash exposures

Few holidays are complete without a visit to a show or an evening entertainment of some kind. Every country has its traditional meal with folk dancing or displays of skill; if you visit as a group, someone may be pulled to their feet to 'join in' with the show and you will naturally want to take pictures. Take a camera with a medium zoom lens (35-70 or even better 28-85mm) and a flashgun. This will not hinder your enjoyment of the evening and should be enough to ensure good pictures.

Be careful to exclude people sitting near you from the bottom of the shot when you take a picture of the show. The flash will illuminate nearby faces or heads far more than the main scene and your exposure will probably be wrong. Stand up, briefly, to take your picture. It can help to pick a seat near a pillar so that you can stand up without obstructing anyone else's view.

Always check the maximum distance on the flashgun calculator scale. You will probably need to set *f*4 or *f*2.8 to photograph a dance show at about 20 feet away; any further than this, and you need a fast ISO 400 film or an extremely powerful flashgun.

Some events take place outdoors and may involve spotlights or self-illuminating

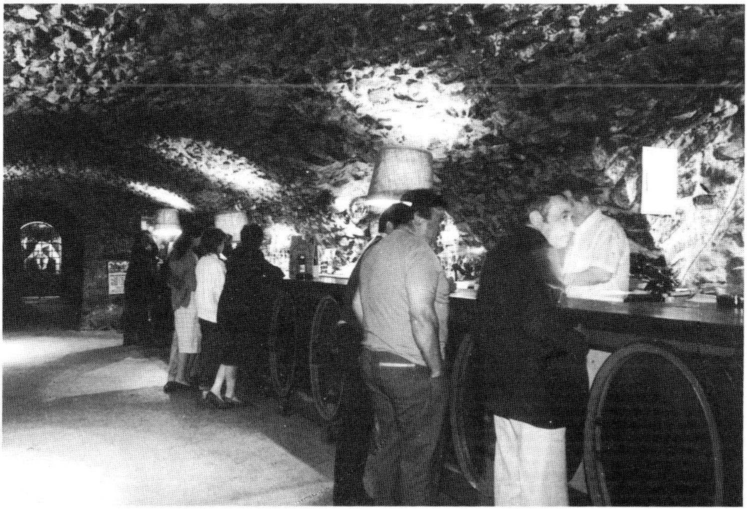

Even at night, people keep still enough to appear in short time exposure shots. There is not much benefit in using a fast film if you find youself using a tripod after dark.

activities like fire-eating. If it is completely dark, always use an ISO 400 film, and set the flash or camera filmspeed setting to ISO 200. Outdoor conditions have the effect of HALVING the normal exposure efficiency of your flash, and this will compensate.

The best time for such pictures is at dusk, when there is still light in the sky, with an exposure carefully balancing natural light and flash. This usually happens without any careful adjustment of the settings – shoot and hope for the best. The effect will be best at wide apertures like *f*2.8. Flash has the additional benefit of freezing the action when the 'available light' shutter speed would be too slow. An exposure of 1/8 at *f*2.8 with flash at dusk, for example, can give an interesting combination of blur and sharpness from a moving subject.

Night-time shots

True night shots need a tripod, and do not often call for fast film. The difference between an ISO 400 film and your normal ISO 100 film is a shift from an exposure of 1/4 of a second to an exposure of one second – as you can not hand-hold EITHER successfully, you need a tripod or

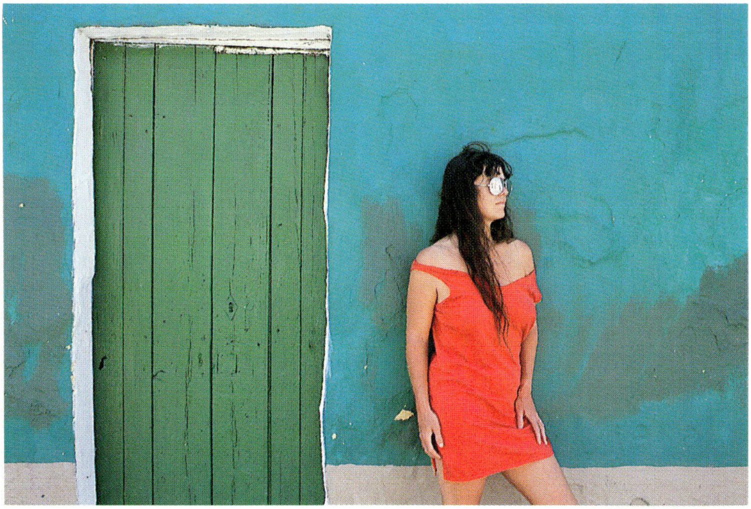

Skin tones look best out of the sun, and against a green or blue background. Try the shady side of the street for a more flattering light and better colours, like this shot of Shirley in Villa Real, Portugal.

camera clamp. Then, it's just as easy to give the one-second exposure. People can only be included in such pictures if they keep very still, and silhouettes often work best.

Subtle effects can be obtained with exposures of about 30 seconds by twilight or moonlight. The colours look very unusual. Gently moving water, with harbour lights reflected, blurs into a smooth sheen; waves become a coloured mist. Resist the temptation to include the moon on such long exposures! Even with a standard 50mm lens, it will become a sausage-shaped arc of light in the sky instead of a circle or crescent moon-shape.

The new fast films, up to ISO 3200, enable candid and action photography in floodlit arenas, street lighting, hotel interiors and most son-et-lumière events. They are extremely grainy. Never let these films be X-rayed, and always buy short rolls (12 or 24 exposures) rather than full 36-exposure films.

Nothing is worse than shooting four or five night-time frames on a film like this and finding you still have it loaded in your camera the next day! Many cameras do not allow you to rewind a cassette without 'losing' the film leader, preventing re-use.

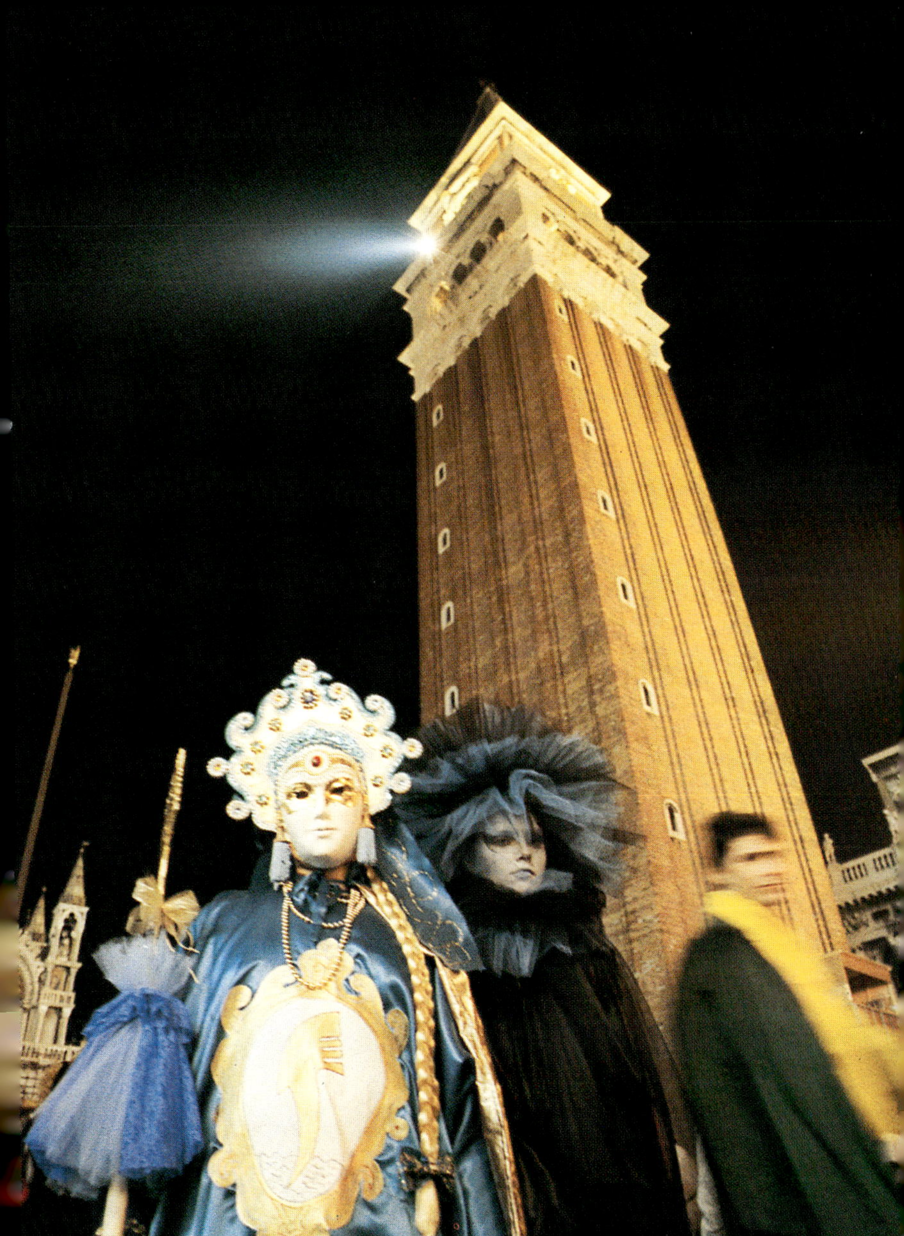

Combining flash with artificial light be an exciting way to get pictures which include people against floodlit backgrounds. Here a 20mm wide-angle has been used with 1s at ƒ8 plus flash on ISO 400 film

BUILT-IN lenses on compact cameras are not the limitation they may seem. As the most popular choice for holiday pictures, the 35mm autofocus compact is also the best – the lens is normally around 35-40mm focal length, giving a good approximation of the normal field of view which most people 'see' by eye.

However, the camera gives equal sharpness to all parts of the scene, unlike the eye which can concentrate on a small area, and many people find its slightly wide-angle view of the world makes many subjects seem small and insignificant. Unless you move in to the closest focusing distance of 1 metre even a head and shoulders portrait is loosely composed and shows more chest, arms and sky than face.

The compact with a fixed lens is ideal for:

* Groups of people

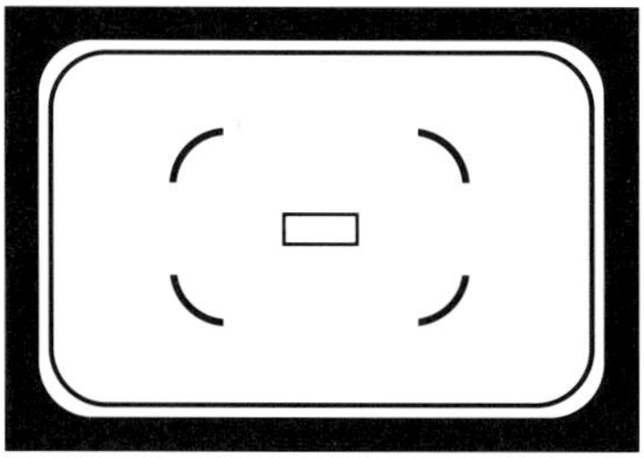

The viewfinder of a low-cost dual-lens compact has the normal central focusing area and a second set of framing marks for the telephoto setting.

* Landscapes and street scenes or markets
* Interiors of larger buildings
* Shots on board boats

Closing in

To overcome the 'distancing' effect of the semi-wide-angle lens on 35mm compacts, many now have either a second so-called tele lens or a zoom. Do not expect cameras like this to photograph a distant subject; the tele or zoom lens simply enlarges the subject to around twice the normal size, and would be called a 'portrait' lens on any other camera. It's equal to the very shortest tele zoom focal length available on 35mm SLRs – 70mm.

The dual lens compacts vary from those fitted with wide-angle and standard options (35mm plus 50mm) to those with more ambitious tele lenses (38mm plus 70mm, for example). The zoom models usually cover a wider range (35mm to 70mm, continuously variable). In all cases you see through the viewfinder a very clear representation of the field of view.

Most dual and zoom lens compacts also have a built-in flash, automatically varying in angle to match the lens, and a close-up facility which lets you shoot flowers, full-face portraits, an unusual dish at a restaurant or colourful fish caught on a boat trip. This feature is really useful and worth paying extra for.

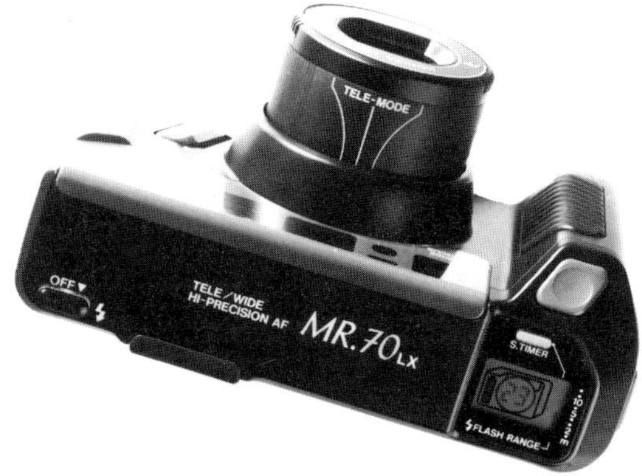

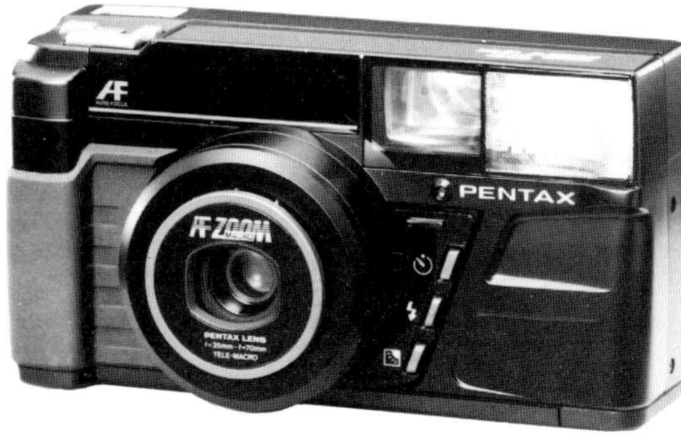

Top: a dual lens compact has a switch which alters the lens setting mechanically. Bottom: a control on the top of this camera, near the shutter, adjusts a motorized 35-70mm zoom to any chosen setting.

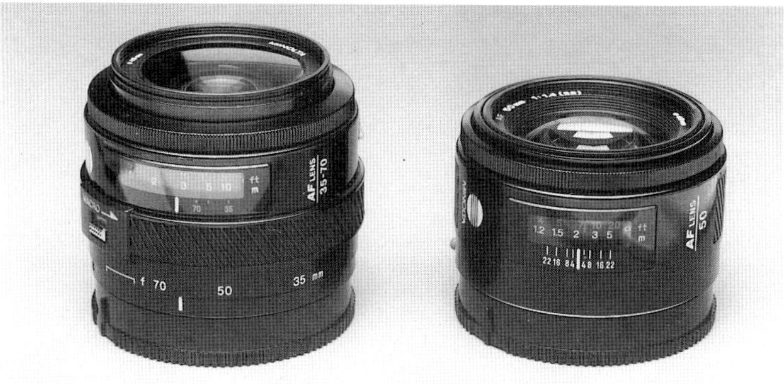

The size and weight of a 35-70mm zoom lens (left) only marginally exceed those of a standard 50mm lens (right), making it the ideal choice for travelling when portability is important.

Single-lens Reflexes

Lenses for SLRs – the popular single-lens reflex camera systems – are easy to try out before you buy. Their effect can be seen very clearly through the viewfinder, but it's hard to judge which choices are best for holiday travel when you try out a lens in a shop.

STANDARD lenses come in two types – the fixed 50mm and the 35-70mm 'standard' zoom, very much like the lens on a zoom compact. While the 50mm offers bright viewing, fine optical quality and small size, the 35-70mm or similar zoom is a far better choice on holiday. If you find light weight and compactness count most, then stick to this type of lens; if you are prepared to carry a slightly heavier camera and do not mind using a large lens all the time, then a 28-85mm, 24-85mm, 35-105mm, 35-135mm or even a 28-135mm can be a fine choice – a whole outfit, depending on your preferences for wide angle and telephoto shooting, in one lens.

Normally you get the best quality, closest focusing distance and largest aperture, hence brightest viewing, with moderate specifications such as 28-85mm or 35-105mm. A 28-135mm may be twice the size of either of them. It is probably best to avoid greater extremes, such as 28-200mm, unless you really need the 'long end' of the lens. In general, any so-called universal zoom lens is always at least as large and heavy as an equivalent telephoto but rarely as good!

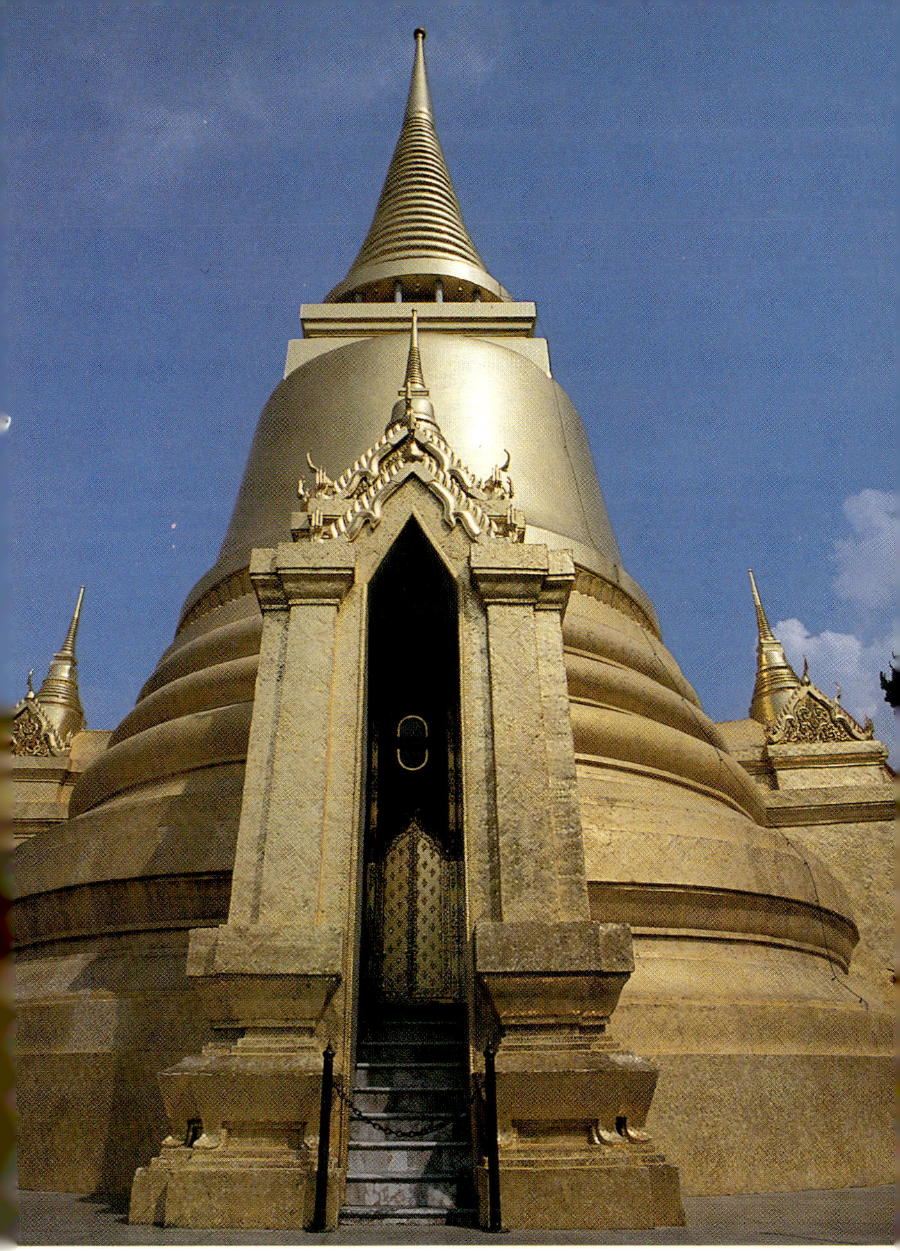

To photograph this Bangkok temple without including many tourists on the steps, a 20mm wide-angle lens was vital. It meant that the whole temple could be photographed from in front of a group of people.

TELEPHOTO zooms, in contrast, are often as good as any similar fixed focal length lens. They make ideal companions in an outfit with a standard zoom, or a standard lens and separate wide-angle. The best value for versatility is a lens of around 70-210mm; there is no real difference between this and an 80-200mm. Buy the best you can afford, and look particularly hard at the maximum aperture (*f*4 or *f*3.5 rather than *f*4.5 or *f*5.6) and the closest normal focusing distance, ignoring any special 'macro' settings. It should be under 1.5 metres.

Some special lightweight tele zooms are ideal for taking on holiday, but they usually have limitations in both the above respects.

One maker offers an autofocus 100-200mm weighing half as much as his 70-210mm, but though small and light, its maximum aperture is *f*4.5 and closest focusing distance 1.9m, compared with *f*4 and 1.1m for the larger lens.

Longer range tele zooms have attractions if you are interested in, say, wildfowl or distant subjects like sailing boats, water skiers and so on. A good specification is 75 or 100mm to 300mm, which is about the limit of telephoto power for hand-holding a camera with normal film in sunshine. The maximum aperture of such lenses, normally *f*5.6, prevents their use in very poor weather.

Wide angles

Wide-angle lenses see more – more of streets, buildings, interiors, groups at close quarters, and more of that deep blue sky. They are indispensable holiday lenses! If you want to get the same views the postcards show, you need at least one wide-angle lens, and the best overall choice is the 28mm. This 'sees' twice as much as the standard 50mm lens. If you own a 35-70mm zoom, a 24mm wide-angle is a better choice; if you own a 28-85mm zoom you already have your wide-angle built in. You might like to try something extreme like a 20mm or 17mm lens, but these are hard to master, though exciting in their dramatic results.

Special lenses

TELEPHOTO (long focus) lenses are specialist lenses today because zooms are so good. The only need for separate telephoto lens is for superb quality or a very large maximum aperture. The 135mm *f*2.8 tele, long familiar, remains an excellent choice for general holiday travel if you don't want a zoom. Fast, wide-aperture 85mm and 100/105mm lenses are more for enthusiasts. There is not much to be gained from carrying a 200mm *f*2.8 or a really long 500mm unless you know your photography very well. Both would be useful on a safari trip, and the 500mm is also super for

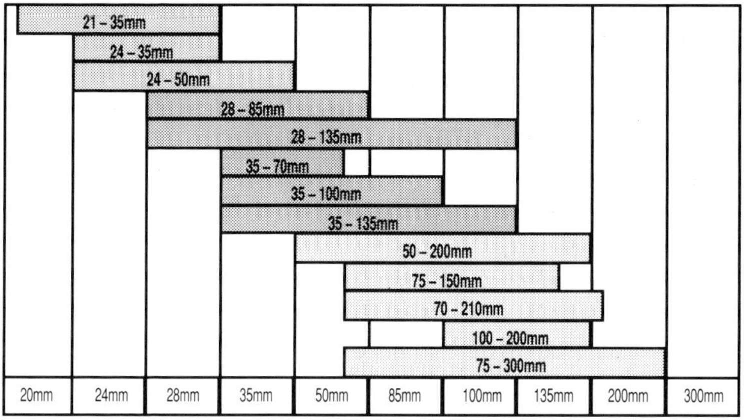

Above: the way that available zoom lenses overlap in their focal lengths allows you to build up a sensible outfit.

sunsets. Neither will be much use on a family holiday .

WIDE ANGLE ZOOMS are an alternative to the standard lens and a separate wide-angle, without the size of standard zooms. Typical ranges include 24-35mm, 24-50mm, and 21-35mm (this is a bulky and expensive type). Wide zooms are often small, have good maximum apertures, and boast excellent performance; they can also be costly. A 24-50mm makes a good companion to a 70-210mm.

ULTRA-WIDE and fisheye lenses, under 20mm in focal length, produce results prone to unwanted visual distortion unless you are aware of how and when to use them. If you just want the occasional optical effect, take a cheap fisheye or superwide adaptor which screws on to the front of your normal lens.

FAST lenses are those with maximum apertures of *f*1.4 or wider (lower *f*-number) with standard and wide-angle lenses, or *f*2.8 and wider with telephotos and zooms. Apart from giving a brighter viewfinder image, they have few advantages for everyday use. The number of times you will ever use the maximum aperture for picture-taking is negligible. The major exceptions are evening or indoor shows and events like bullfights, equestrian displays, theatre and barbecues. You will gain more by taking a roll or two of high speed film (ISO 1000) than by purchasing a 100mm *f*2 lens and sticking to ISO 100 film!

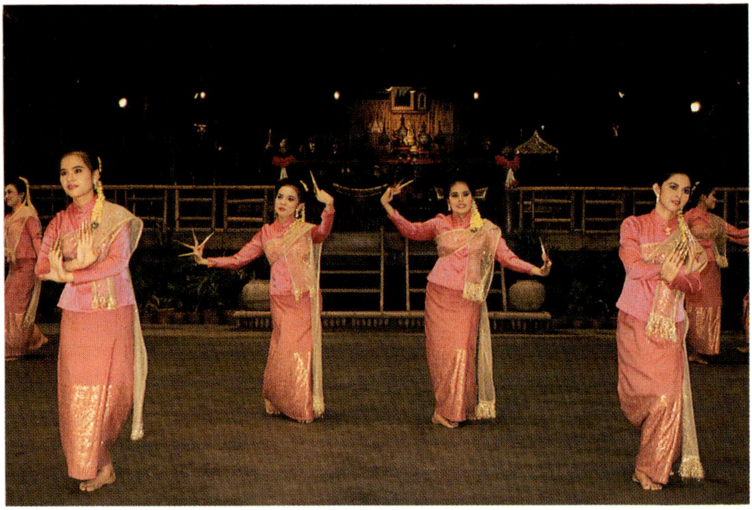

A very fast lens allows low-light shooting, but a fast film like the ISO 400 used above is a better solution. A macro lens focuses very close and gives critical sharpness to studies of texture at any distance (right).

MACRO lenses are special standard 50mm or 100mm 'tele' lenses which focus to life-size (or thereabouts) on film. With one of these lenses you can switch from a distant landscape to a single wildflower. They are ideal for holidays with natural history, art, architecture, gardening, antiques, geology or similar interests.

Other special lenses include 'mirror' telephotos, lightest in weight for wildlife and zoo photographs, and 'apo' tele lenses which produce the sharpest long-distance colour images. You can also buy special 'perspective control' lenses for taking purely architectural pictures. All these specialist lenses cost a great deal as so few are sold each year. They are not essential for good holiday photography unless you have very specialized skills.

The ideal outfit

The whole set of lenses you own makes your outfit. It may be just one simple lens – a 35-70mm zoom. It may be four or five lenses – a 20mm, a 28mm, a 50mm, a 70-210mm and a 400mm telephoto. The ideal outfit for most people seems to be two or three lenses, sometimes with a spare camera body.

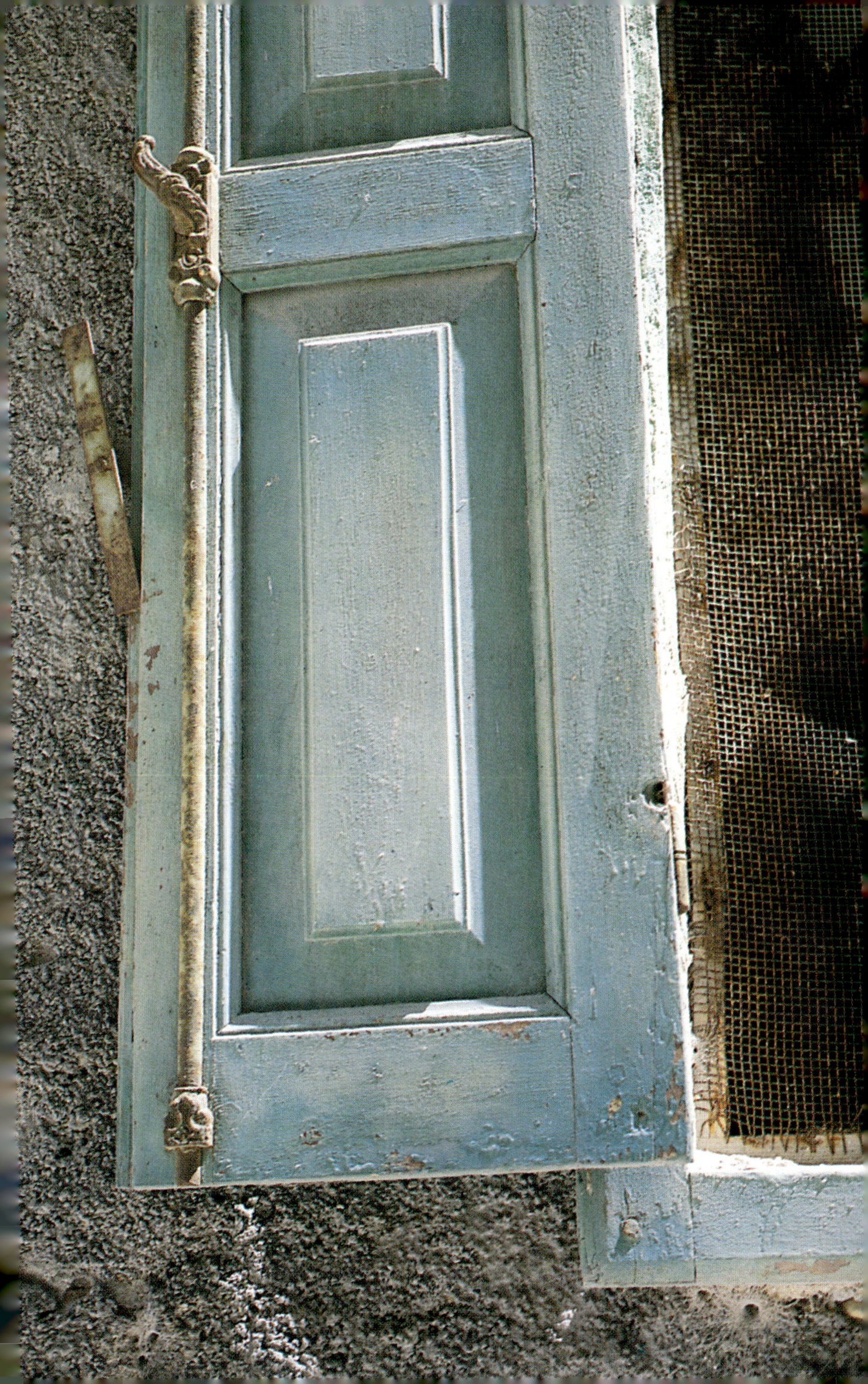

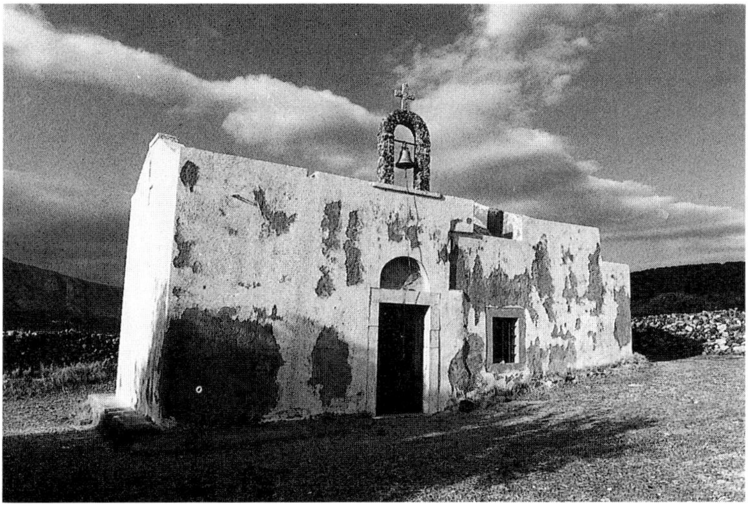

Spacing the focal lengths is important. An outfit with a 50mm, a 135mm and a 70-210mm zoom has no wide-angle ability and a duplication of the 135mm focal length. One with a 28mm, a 35mm and 50mm has no telephoto ability and is very closely spaced. Good combinations include:

* 28mm, 50mm and 70-210mm
* 24-50mm and 70-210mm
* 24mm and 35-135mm
* 28mm and 50-200mm
* 24mm, 35-70mm, and 75-300mm

Weight matters too; the standard 50mm and ordinary 28mm weigh little, so the bulk of a 70-210mm is acceptable. Carry a 21-35mm, 28-135mm and 75-300mm and you will soon know the difference. Moreover, not one of these three lenses is small enough to be unobtrusive. The all-zoom outfit will be heavy, cost twice as much, and be far harder to pack into a small camera hold-all, and may kill your enthusiasm for holiday photography.

Even if you don't mind the encumbrance of a heavy outfit, your family and friends will...

The wide-angle lens, top, includes more sky and allows a close viewpoint. In this case, a tree would have obscured the building from further away.

A 135mm telephoto (right) gives an ideal perspective for street scenes and general landscapes, especially with figures.

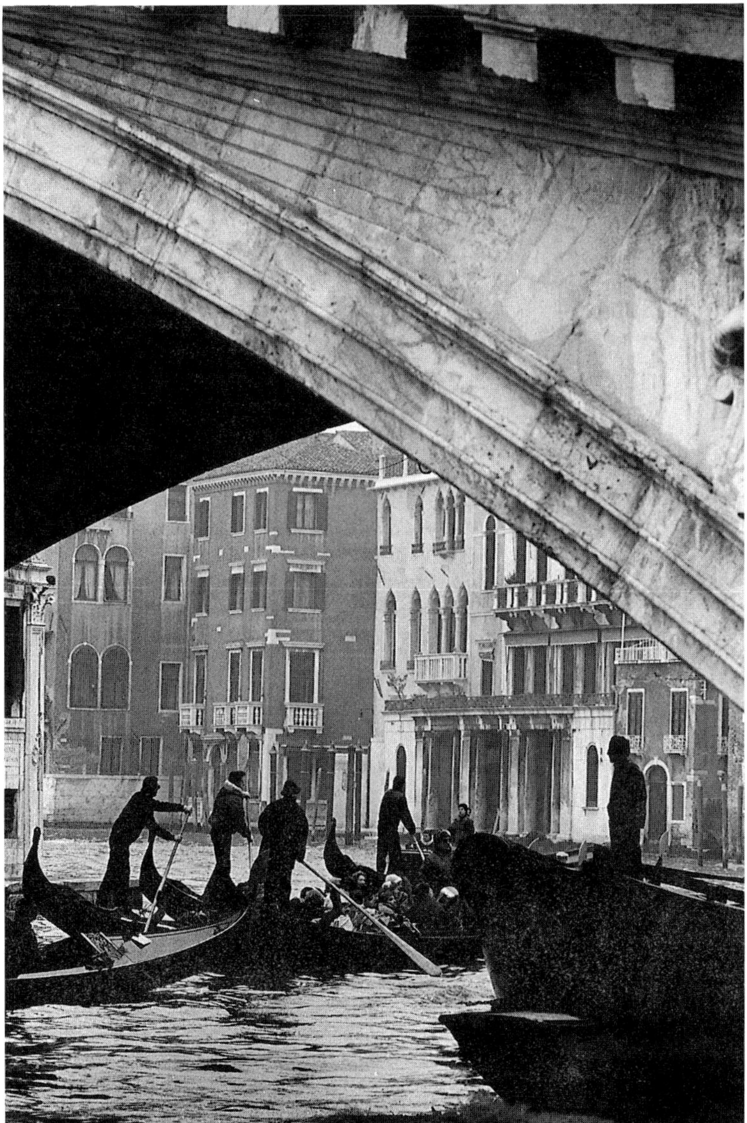

Lenses for subjects

What is your main interest? Some lenses are ideal for some subjects:

LANDSCAPES
28, 24-35, or 50mm
70-210 or 75-300mm
85, 100, 135, or 200mm

GENERAL SCENIC
28 or 24-35mm
28-85 or 28-135mm
35-70 or 35-105mm,
35-135, 85 or 100mm

PEOPLE
35, 24-50, or 50mm
35-70 or 35-105mm
70-150 or, 70-210mm
85 or 100mm

EVENTS
24, 28 or 24-50mm
28-85 or 28-135mm
70-210mm
85, 100 or 135mm

CRAFTS
28, 35 or 24-35mm
50mm standard
35-70 or 28-85mm
75-150 or 85mm

ARCHITECTURE
20, 24, 28 or 35mm
50mm standard
85, 100, 135 or 200mm

INTERIORS
20, 24, 28 or 35mm
24-35, 24-50 or 50mm
28-85mm, 28-135mm

GARDENS AND FLOWERS
28, 35 or 24-50mm
50 or 100mm macro
70-210mm zoom with macro

ACTION SPORTS
28 or 24-50mm
28-135 or, 35-135mm
70-210 or 75-300mm
100, 135 or 200mm
300mm and over

NATURAL HISTORY
28, 35 or 24-50mm
50 or 100mm macro
70-210 or 75-300mm
135, 200 and 300mm+

NIGHT-TIME
28 or 35mm
50mm standard
Any lens faster than *f*2
35-70 or 28-85mm
85, 100 or 135mm

SAFARIS
24 or 24-50mm
28-135 or 35-135mm
70-210 or, 75-300mm
135, 200 and 300mm+

MOUNTAINEERING
28 or 24-50mm
50mm standard
28-85 or 35-105mm
75-150mm
85, 100 or 135mm

AERIAL PHOTOGRAPHS
35mm
50mm standard
85, 100 or 135mm
35-135mm zoom

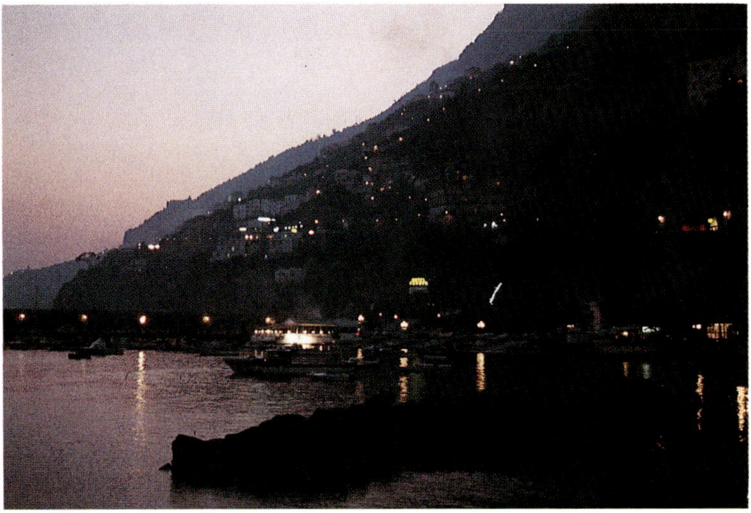

Dusk and night photography naturally calls for a tripod, but the shot above was taken hand-held using ISO 1000 film. Below: the standard lens is ideal for candid shots like this quick portrait of a Hong Kong mother and baby.

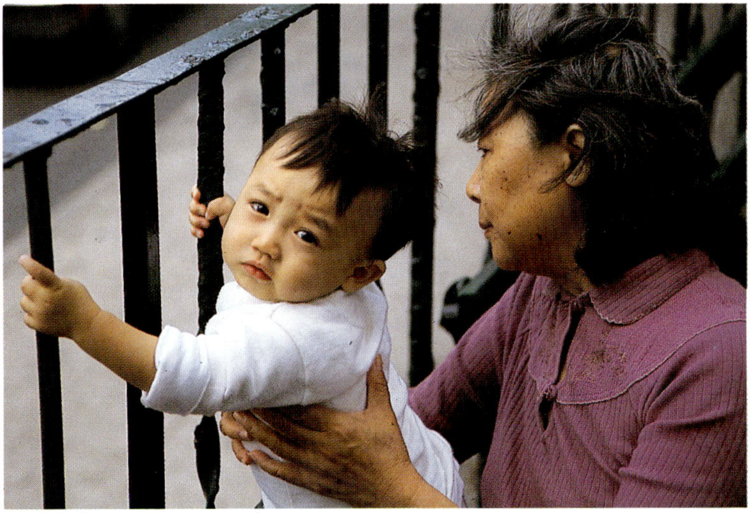

5: GREEN LANDSCAPES

THE COLOURS of temperate countries – green landscapes – are more vivid than those of many places we visit to enjoy the sun. Although bright sunshine gives the impression of colour and many artefacts and buildings are more colourful in hot countries, a European spring or autumn has far more depth and saturation of colour. The problem lies in getting this on to film, and the techniques are important.

First of all, if you travel in temperate areas you should always travel at the right time. Many photographers put away their cameras for a couple of months in late summer; July and August are often hazy and the colours of foliage are either darkened by age or obscured by dust. Late July in the South of France is not an ideal time for photography, whereas early June or late September are normally both good times to choose.

If you plan holidays the way that we do, then the warmer destinations are reserved for early or late season. We will look at the Mediterranean in this context later. From June to August you have a fair chance of good weather in most of Europe and the northern parts of America and Japan. The same applies to southern Australia and northern New Zealand from December to March. There are many other places which have essentially green landscapes, but at other times of year; much of Northern India from November to March, for example. Study the average temperature and rainfall guides and do not always go for the driest, hottest period if you want good pictures!

Countries vary

The best periods for scenic photography in Britain and Northern Europe (including Scandinavia) are from early May to mid-June, and late August to the end of September. The further north you go, the later the seasons run; Spring colours in Italy are best captured in April, while in Scotland you can wait until June.

If you can, head for western and southern coastlines and hilly or mountainous areas rather than eastern or northern shores and flat countryside. The weather variations on a western coast produce more interesting light. One of the best areas for photography is the west of Scotland where the clarity of the air and the quality of light can almost be guaranteed, even if the temperature can not.

Inland in Europe, look for areas with lakes and strong contours; avoid industrial areas and conurbations. A good example of very unphotogenic scenery can be found by cruising up the Rhine; it is hard to get many decent pictures even in the most famous areas. Do the same journey by car and drive a few kilometres away from the river itself and you can find an infinite variety of scenes.

The best-known areas for photography in the United States and Canada tend to be major tourist attractions – from New England to the Rockies. It is uncertain whether Disneyland and similar attractions are really photogenic, or just interesting to snap. For green landscapes, the northern states and coastal areas as well as mountain ranges are the best destinations. Although the desert blooms very colourfully, you've got to be there at exactly the right time.

Apart from the scale of the landscape, the United States provides particularly well for pictures of historical interest. Re-creations of early towns with costumed actors, perfectly restored areas, and ensuring that mess and modernity do not interfere make American theme parks and heritage sites excellent for picture-taking.

The countryside in Japan is as green and scenic as anywhere in Europe and closely resembles familiar farmland and mountain scenery. Access to it is NOT guaranteed on any package trips and very few Japanese live in the hills; earthquake dangers restrict development to a few areas. The holidaymaker will be pointed in the direction of major shrines and parks, which are superb subjects in their own right. It can pay to take a tripod because many of the best Japanese subjects are indoors, and photography is allowed nearly everywhere.

In the north of India and in Kashmir and Nepal the scenery can be very European in feel during the rainy season, but here the interest for most holidaymakers lies in cultural differences, so you will be more likely to photograph the towns and people. In contrast, a trip to New Zealand will be much like a trip to the Scottish Highlands – you will be on the lookout for landscapes.

More adventurous travel, going beyond the bounds of normal holidaymaking, is less of a risk photographically if you join a specialist photographic tour. A group may be organized to arrive in the right part of Canada just when the maple trees are at their best colour, or to visit Thailand before the streets flood and immobilize the traffic. This is the best way to travel if you are not familiar with weather conditions and the changing seasons.

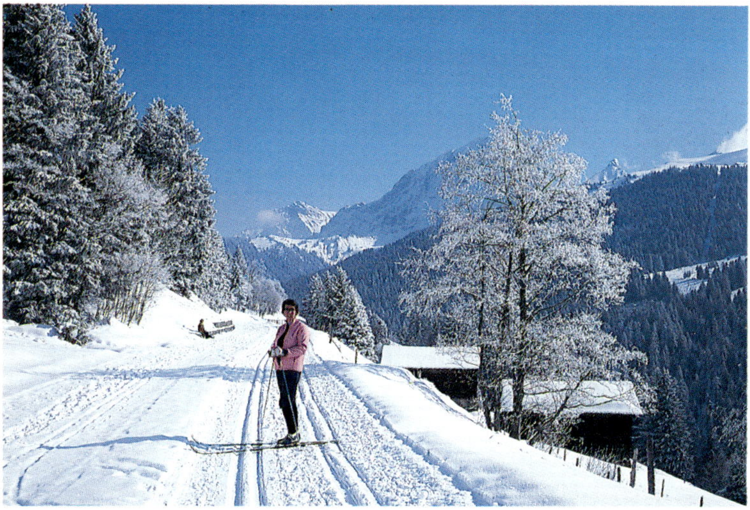

Winter photography is best in countries with both snow and sunshine – photograph by Derek Grossmark. In Mediterranean climates (right) visit in spring to capture colourful flowers instead of summer dust.

The seasons

Seasonal differences bring most changes to the colours of the landscape. The quality of light may be identical in spring and autumn, but the colours will be from a different palette.

WINTER is a good season for photography if snow is common in the area you are visiting, or if you are in a country location. Winter is a bad time in cities and towns because the buildings create such dense shadows in low sunshine. The same low sun gives texture to landscapes and exposed buildings such as country churches. Colours can often be surprisingly clean, bright and fresh.

SPRING has the advantage of pure colour. Leaves are not just a brighter green – they are thinner, so that the sun can shine through them from behind, and they have not developed the waxy coating which gives older leaves a dull sheen. When foliage is young, more light can penetrate in woodlands; subjects seen through trees will show more detail. Flowers are at their best in late spring and early summer. Agricultural areas offer the benefit of young animals in the fields.

EARLY SUMMER is a good time to shoot distant landscapes,

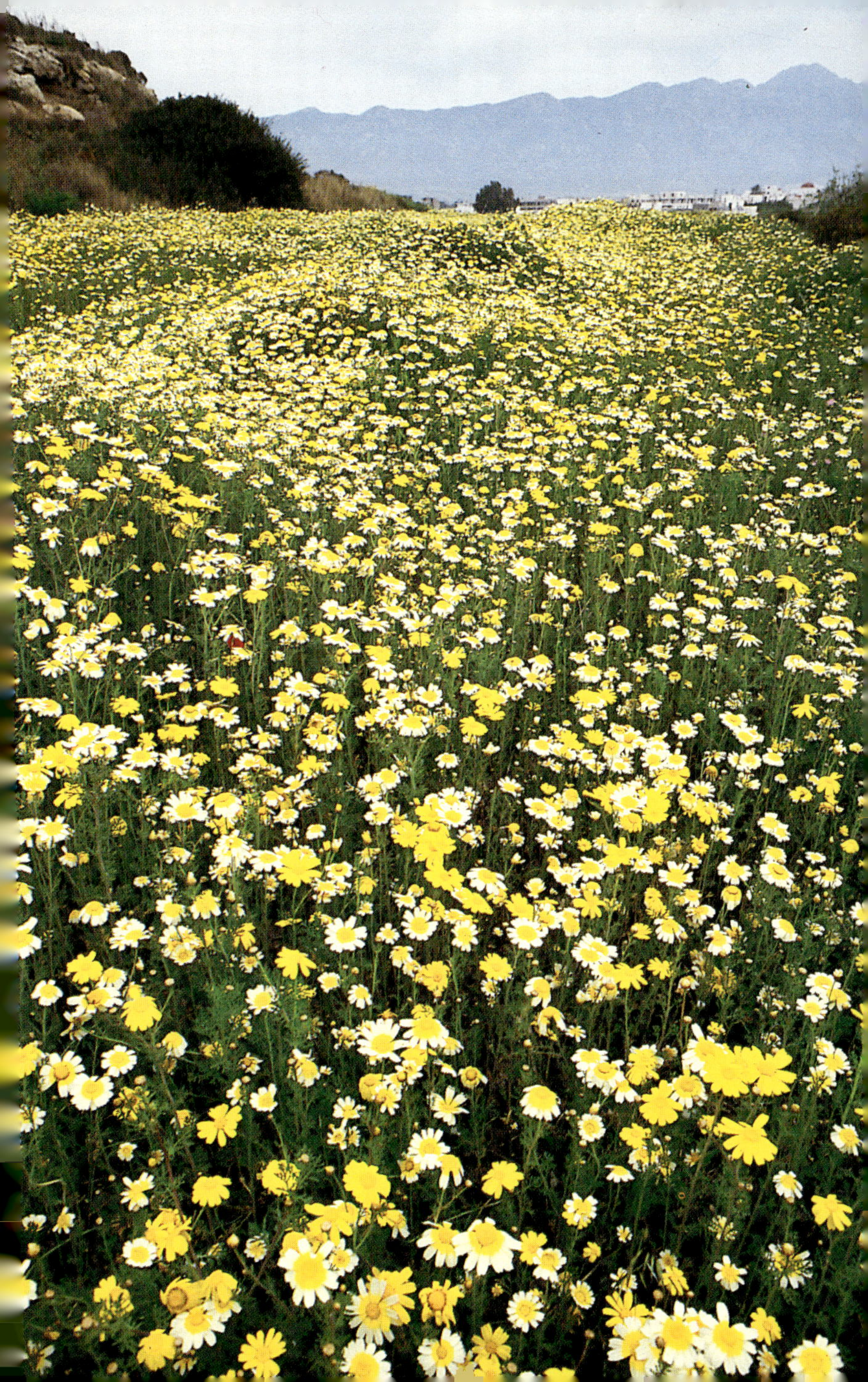

with full leaf cover and a good bright green in the grass and trees, creating contrasts in mixed deciduous and conifer forests. You have the benefit of long evenings in many areas, with good sunsets following an hour or more of late evening sun, which is often very warm in colour.

HIGH SUMMER is not as good for colours. Overhead sun is not the best light to shoot in, and the darker greens do not record well on most films – they tend to look blue-green rather than bright green. In many areas humidity rises and produces aerial haze which makes the distant scene bluish and deadens the overall quality of light. Once again, the best colours will be produced when the sun is low. The old advice about shooting before 10.00am and after 4.00pm is good advice! In central Europe August is a good month for scenic photography because of the harvest, and the traditional hayricks which create patterns across the fields.

For many holidaymakers this has advantages. You can sunbathe or swim in the middle of the day, and go sightseeing and taking photographs in the late afternoon and evening.

AUTUMN has many of the benefits of spring. The leaves become translucent again, and lose their sheen, changing colour to yellows which are as bright as the fresh greens of new foliage. Many other colours appear, including some vivid reds and browns, and the patchwork of fields becomes fascinating because mature crops alternate with fresh ploughing and second growths of new grass just as bright as in springtime.

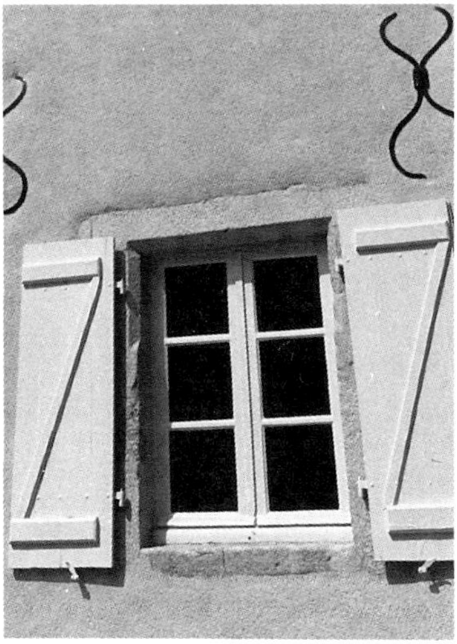

Above – high summer sun is not always an ideal light. Right – the low angle sun of spring and autumn produces better texture and tonal range.

It is in autumn that the difference between green landscapes and Mediterranean landscapes is most apparent. Where the summer has turned entire islands to shades of brown further south, autumn simply returns colour to the scenery in places like southern Austria, northern Spain or central France.

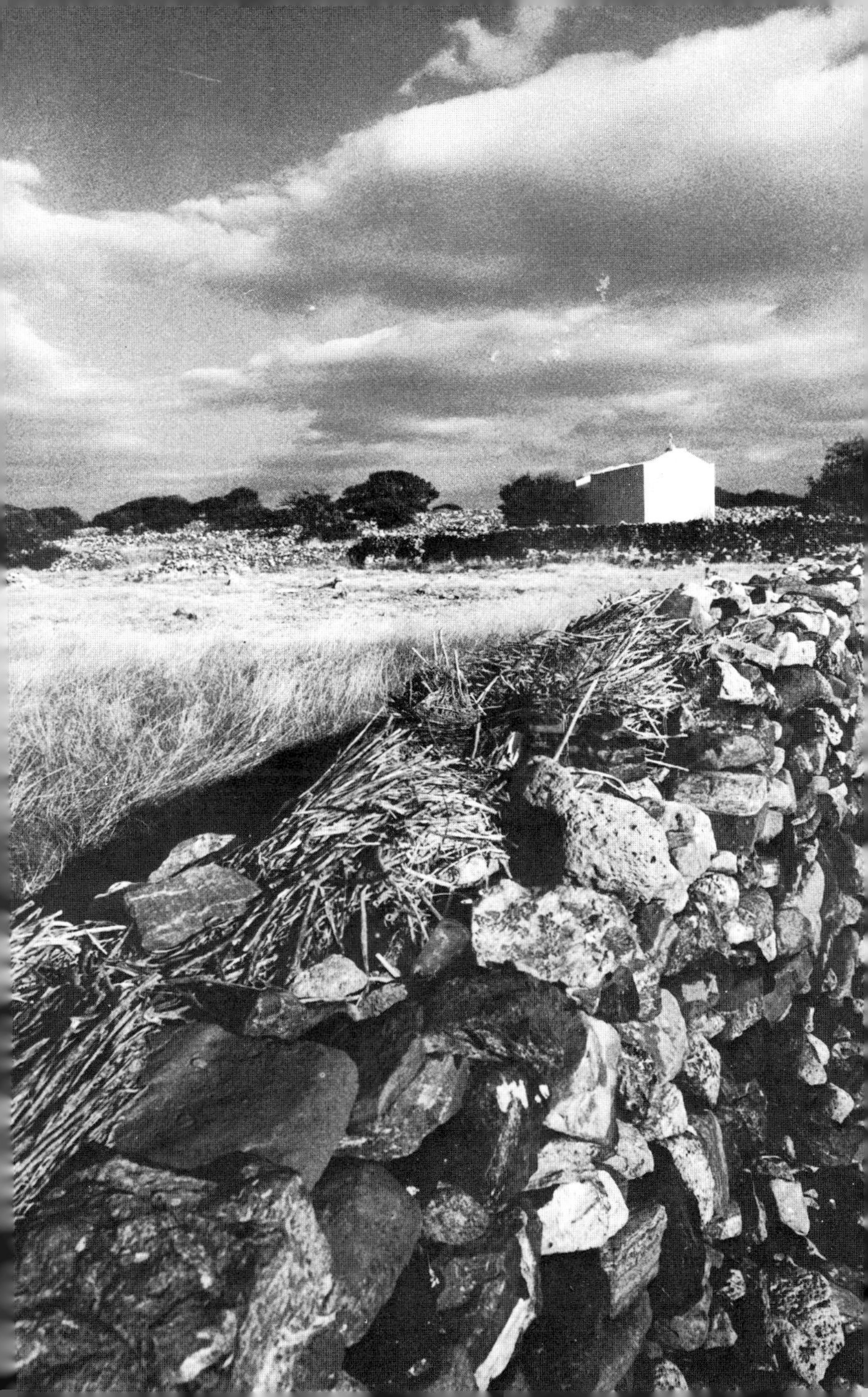

Subjects

All green landscapes tend to look much the same unless you search out interesting subjects. A valley in Wales can look like a glen in Scotland and a lake with pine forests looks the same the world over. It is very important to find good foreground interest to make your shots different.

Try to show things typical of the place you have visited. In France, for example, you can place a vineyard in the foreground of a general view. In Holland you would look for tulip-fields, a canal or perhaps a windmill to figure in your composition. People in the landscape add interest, especially if you can place them prominently.

Barns, old farms and churches look different in every country. Rather than just photographing a landscape with fields and hills, find a view which includes a village in the middle distance and a church spire characteristic of the region. If there is a distinctive local pattern of wall-building or an old farming method, show it. Above all avoid pictures which give no clues to their location and simply show another pretty scene.

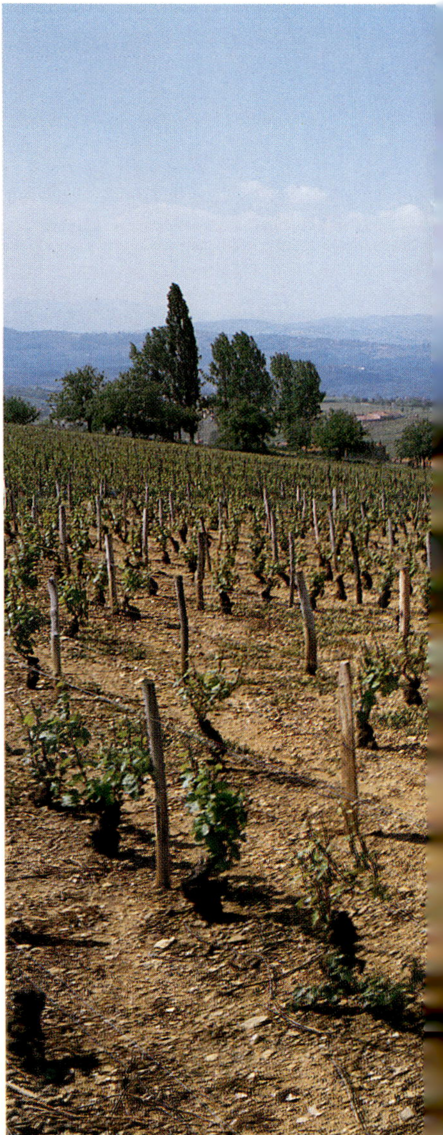

A landscape in the Beaujolais hills of France would be nothing without vineyards. Always include the most appropriate foreground you can in your scenic photographs.

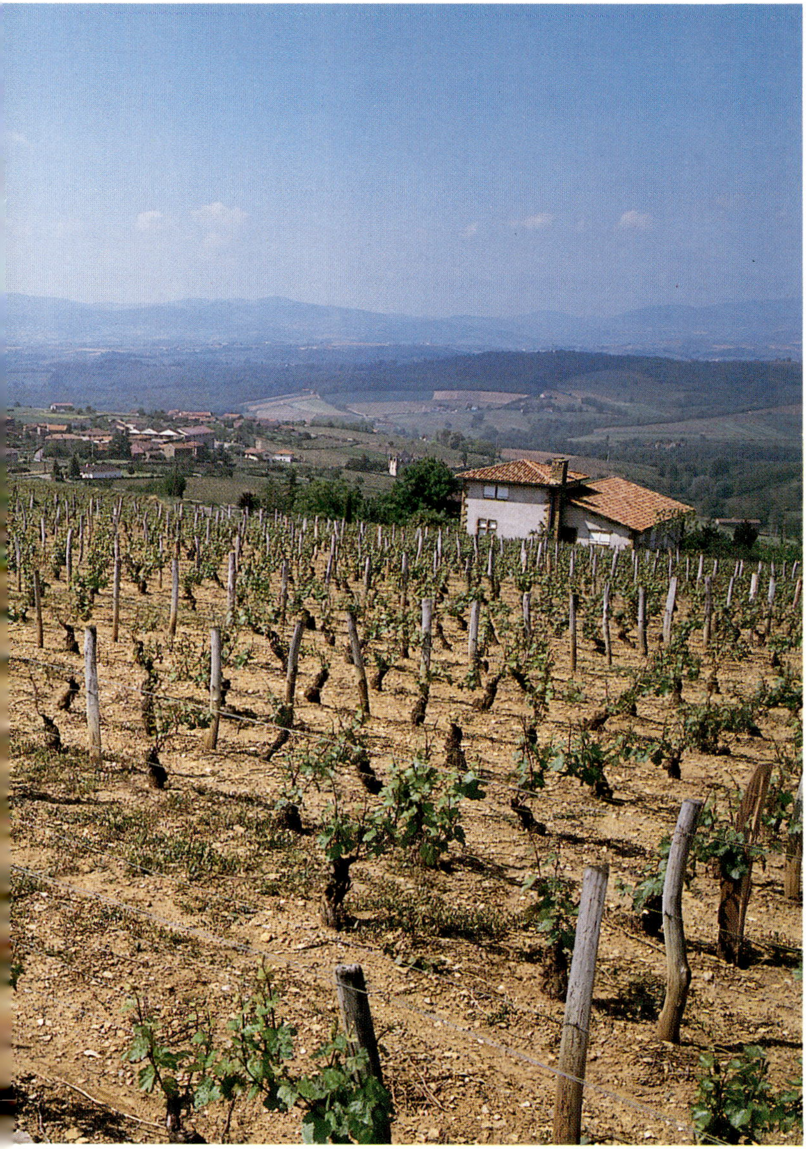

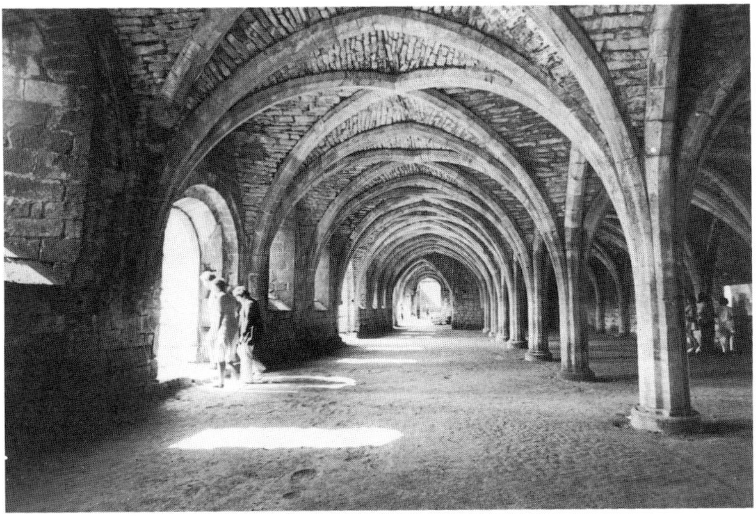

A medium-speed film is best for quality and can be used in all conditions, including dimly-lit interiors if you take a lightweight tripod or camera clamp with you.

Film and light

For general photography in temperate areas, a film which will show off colours to their best is recommended – and this means a slow or medium-speed film. Do not use ISO 200 or 400 all the time; use ISO 100, or slower in colour slides. Inland, you may find problems, with low light levels in winter and towards the end of the day. Some of the best lighting conditions occur close to sunset and you may find yourself using settings like 1/30th at $f4$ with ISO 100 film.

The solution is to TAKE WITH YOU a lightweight tripod, mini-pod or monopod. Any one of these will help you stabilize your camera when long exposures are needed. Whereas a tripod is not necessary on a beach holiday because of the general levels of light, it is a necessity as soon as you enter woodlands in the evening.

The pictures you obtain using a tripod will be much better than shots taken by switching to a faster film when the light begins to fail. Landscapes do not move unless there is a strong wind, which probably means unsuitable light, and people are surprisingly good at keeping still for a fraction of a second.

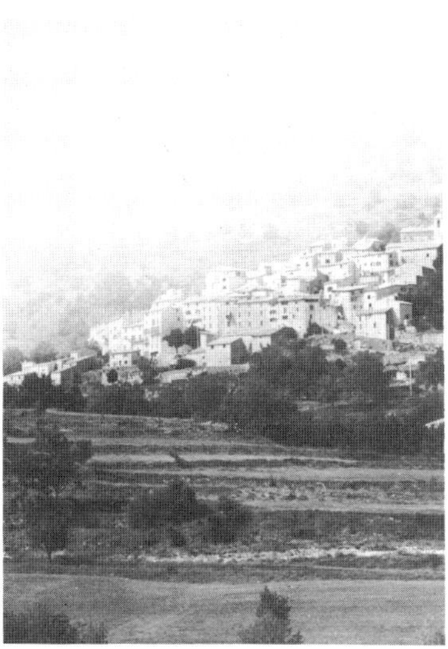

Above: a shot without a haze filter shows little distant detail. Below: clarity WITH the filter.

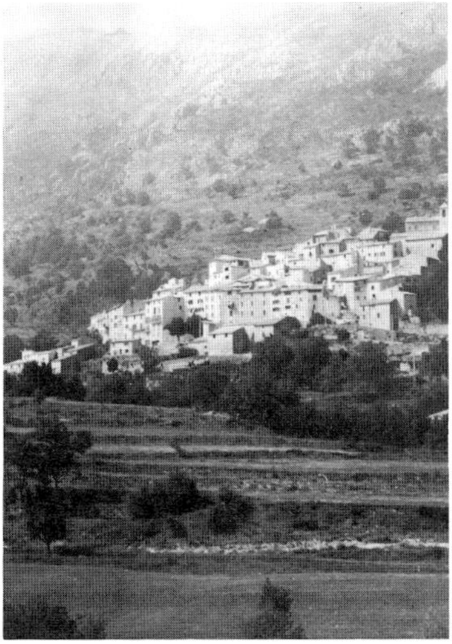

Vital filters

There are two filters you must use for landscape photography, particularly in spring and autumn. One is the UV-Haze filter (or Skylight 1A, which is equally suitable) and the second is a polarizer.

The haze filter is used on the lens at all times. Apart from protecting the glass front element, it reduces blue haze in the distance which can not always be seen by eye, but would otherwise be recorded on film. Without the filter, your panoramic landscapes may not be as clear as you saw them at the time.

The polarizing filter is even more useful. Because it will cause an equivalent light loss to using a much slower film, do not leave it fitted all the time. It has wide-ranging effects on most photographs and can spoil portraits by producing an unpleasant skin tone and texture. With landscape scenes it is invaluable. Do not think that a polarizer will always deepen blue sky or cut reflections from water; this depends on many factors, including the rotation of the polarizer. Generally, it will penetrate aerial haze even better than the UV-Haze filter, and it will greatly brighten up the colours of foliage.

It does this by 'seeing through' the sheen on the surface of leaves and grass to reveal the saturated colours underneath. Spring and

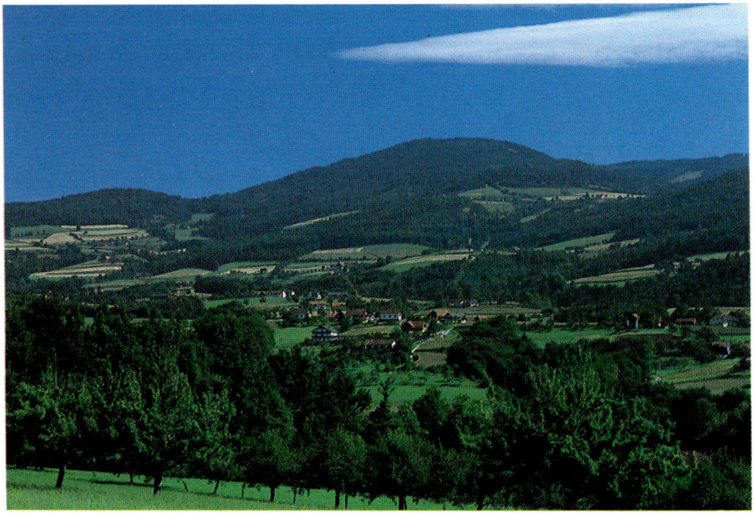

A polarizer, above, gives brilliant colours to this landscape in Styria, Austria, above. The sky has a naturally pure blue which responds well to the filter at this time of day.

autumn scenes photographed with a polarizer have the brilliant colours you see in calendar and postcard shots. Try to avoid eliminating reflections from lakes (water can look empty and black if polarized incorrectly) but use your polarizer on green scenes to improve the colour.

Evening light

Landscapes are also greatly improved by evening light. The colours seem far brighter. This is simply because the colour temperature of evening sun is warmer with a higher proportion of yellow. Anything yellow, green, orange, red or brown will appear brighter in this light – and these happen to be the main colours of nature. The sky opposite the low sun stays blue, of course. Blue has the highest degree of contrast with warm colours, and the result is exactly what a photographer needs. Morning light is rarely as effective because aerial haze tends to reduce contrast, though on some days the light after dawn is worth all the effort of getting up early. The problem is KNOWING that it will be like that in order to plan your alarm call – with evening light you can anticipate the likely conditions.

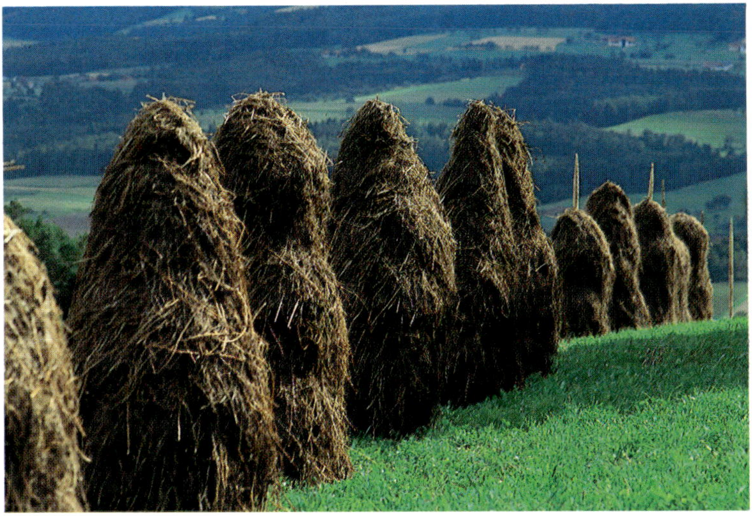

Later in the day, the light is warmer in colour, with deeper shadows. The sky would no longer look blue near the horizon, and has been cropped entirely out of this picture to emphasize the composition.

Bad weather

This brings us to genuine bad weather. The risk you take in holidaying in any green country is the reason why there's so much green around – rain, fog, mist or even snow. The good photographer takes advantage of conditions even if all around curse them. Few scenes look good in solid rain, but storms crossing valleys and hills create exceptional photo opportunities.

Stormy light in the evening or at sunset, with heavy grey clouds behind brilliantly lit scenery or buildings, provides the most dramatic and beautiful setting for photography. You may be lucky enough to have wet rocks or streets and even a rainbow set against a dark sky... If this happens, don't just sit in the bar watching. Wait for a break in the rain and get out there!

Close-ups of wet leaves, reflections in puddles, views mirrored in flooded fields, solitary figures with umbrellas; all these things can produce superb pictures.

Fog is destructive to photography if thick, but mist can produce fine results if you walk into woodlands or select prominent silhouetted foreground subjects. The sun breaking

Clouds over the sun don't spell an end to photography. Have a look at the town or countryside despite the conditions. You may find many good subjects and more dramatic lighting.

through mist produces interesting light. Often you can drive or walk to a higher point and look down on mist, which turns out to be low cloud, drifting in brilliant white sunlit swathes in a valley below. In hilly country it's always worth remembering this.

Winter does not mean bad weather. Dull light on a snow scene is very disappointing, and perhaps the camera should be put away unless you have colourfully dressed people to photograph close-up. You simply have to think differently when conditions are genuinely poor, and look for interiors, dusk scenes with lights, close-ups and so on.

Exposure problems

There are two main exposure problems in conventional landscape photography. In conditions of low sunshine, early or late in the day or in winter, you may encounter very dense shadows and high contrast. The secret of successful pictures under these conditions is to avoid large areas of shadow showing in the picture (no more than one-third of the picture content) and base your exposure on the fully-lit parts of the shot. You can do this by using spot metering or taking a close-up reading in the sunlit area.

In the opposite conditions, on a dull day with a plain white sky and drab foreground area, you may end up with much the same problem; the sky is just too bright and white compared with the dark foreground. Here, assume that as the sky is already plain white it does not matter. The best thing to do is to exclude it from the picture by using a different angle, or at least keeping it to a minimum area by aiming the camera downwards. Doing either of these things eliminates a potential exposure error. If you want a large area of white sky to appear in the shot, base your exposure reading on the ground or subject detail alone, and re-compose the picture after holding or locking in this reading.

Maximum quality

The secret of successful photography in green landscapes is to achieve colour saturation, clarity and tonal range. All the advice so far will help you do this, but to sum up:

* Use a medium-speed or slow film
* If necessary, take a tripod with you
* Fit a UV-Haze filter as standard
* Use a polarizing filter on most sunlit views
* Look for late afternoon or evening light
* Compose with strong foregrounds
* Expose for the *highlights* in sunshine, and for the main *subject-area* on dull days

6: MEDITERRANEAN HOLIDAYS

MEDITERRANEAN countries – and any others with similar climates and surroundings – are popular with photographers. Fashion catalogues send photographic teams to Spain, North Africa, Italy, France and Greece despite uncertain weather. The architecture and landscape are deciding factors.

Much of the Mediterranean area features limestone, marble, and whitewashed walls, often with terracotta-tiled roofs. The streets are dusty or sandy and foliage is often silver-green with plenty of flowers from spring to autumn. Tropical and equatorial sun passes directly overhead with only a brief sunset and twilight; whereas Mediterranean sun only gets 'too high' for good pictures in midsummer and the sunset and twilight are both long enough to allow time for a variety of pictures.

Civilization makes places photogenic. Old townscapes, rambling up hillsides, look better than modern villages; a few centuries can add texture, colour and consistency to stonework and cultivated land. Traditional dress and old-fashioned farming methods are attractive as well as interesting. A herd of goats on a hillside forms a constantly-moving pattern, olive trees grow in their own distinctively gnarled way, fishing boats are painted brightly every spring... These are the details which make the Mediterranean photogenic.

Seasonal variety

For visitors from Europe and North America the Mediterranean has the advantage of synchronous seasons. Spring may come earlier in Spain than in England, but it does come when an English visitor expects to find it. All the seasons are earlier than in countries further north, and winter is often unexpectedly colourful as far as flowers and fields go.

The times to avoid are high summer, from late June to the end of August, and mid-winter, from late November to February. Greek islands do not have a cold winter and snow is almost unknown, but fierce winds keep the fishing fleets in port over the Christmas period. In more northern places like Venice snow is common as late as March.

Some places have short spells of local weather which you should avoid. The coastal areas of the south of France and northern Italy suffer from the 'mistral' wind in winter and flat, lifeless colours in midsummer because of high humidity. The Balearic islands experience the wind as the 'tramontana'.

Generally you should visit southern Mediterranean areas like Tunisia, Malta, Cyprus, Israel and the Costa del Sol in April or May if photography is your main objective. Central and northern areas like Majorca, Naples, Corfu, Venice or Arles are best left until

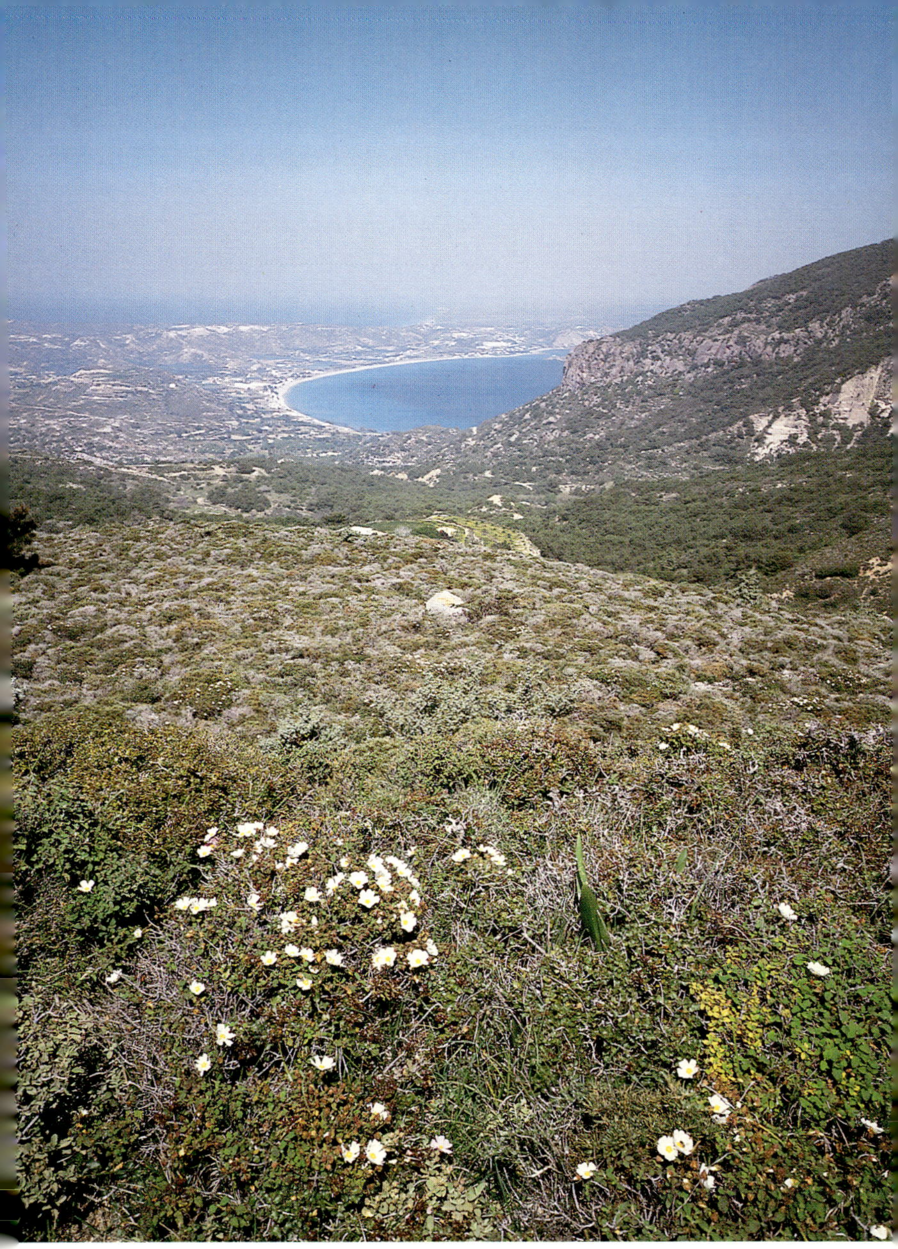

Spring on a Greek island: each island has its own character, and in the case of Kos the scenery can be almost alpine. Herbs and alpine flowers grow high up to provide a foreground for a wide-angle view.

June. Late September and October, with the sea and land thoroughly warmed by two or three months of sunshine, are good throughout the area – but by then the spring colours will have been bleached by summer, the boats and houses will have lost the freshness of their annual coat of paint, and the beaches may be littered with rubbish.

Local variety

Most tourist countries have rules which can affect photography. In Greece no road-mending or house-building work can take place in the tourist season in many areas, so winter becomes a hive of activity coinciding with rainfall. Few places look photogenic and most of the waste is dumped on the beaches. Early in spring all this work stops, the houses are re-painted, and the rubbish is bulldozed deep beneath the sand.

School holidays can make or break your attempts to capture traditional town scenes. Streets with a couple of old ladies in black adding a graphic element change to streets full of teenagers on small motorcycles. Some holiday areas (again in Greece) become the destination for state holidays for city schoolchildren.

Study your travel brochures. Unexpectedly low-cost weeks or an extension of the 'low' season often have reasons like this behind them. It can be better to pay extra and go a couple of weeks later when all the villages are back to normal and tidied up. On the other hand, you might find the work of painting the houses a good subject.

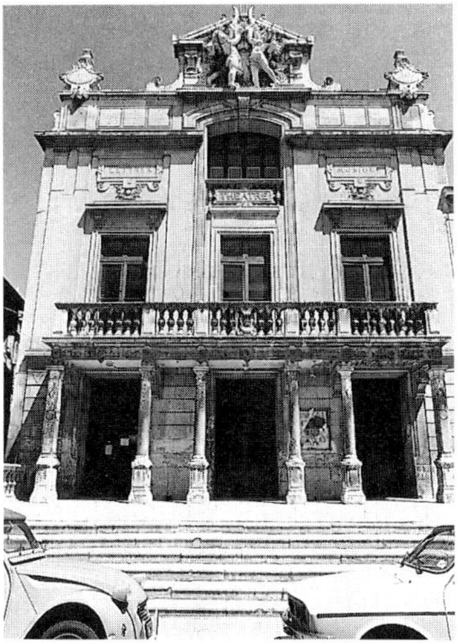

French Provençal façades call for a wide-angle lens and are rarely seen from a distance.

Architecture

The characteristic architecture of a city like Naples demands completely different equipment from that of (for example) the nearby Amalfi coast resorts. Historic cities, with major cathedrals and buildings several stories high on flat ground, are difficult to photograph well without a good wide-angle lens.

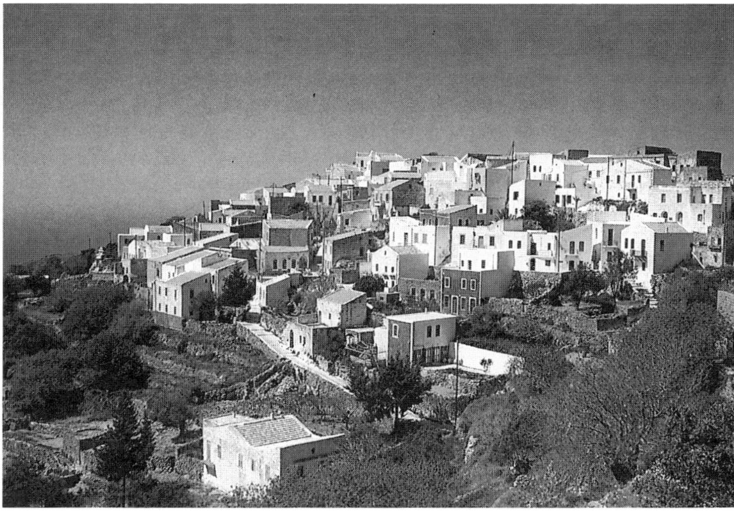

Hillside villages abound in the Mediterranean. They are best photographed from the next hill with a standard or telephoto lens, and hardly ever look impressive at street level.

Hillside villages are on a smaller scale. At street level, an ordinary standard lens is often the best choice, and the whole village can be photographed with a standard or long focus lens from the next hill or a convenient viewpoint on the road.

Greek and North African churches and mosques often have beautiful domes, sometimes painted a rich blue. From ground level they have no impact; climb to a higher level (as you nearly always can) and the dome will look much better from above. Any terraced village on a hillside will look at its best from a distance, seen from an similar or slightly higher level, with a lens around 135-200mm.

Interiors of Mediterranean churches and palaces can be very dark in contrast to the brilliant light outside. Your camera's meter will cope with this even if your eyes do not. Spot metering helps to avoid excessive influence from bright windows.

There are some places which are worth visiting for architecture alone, whether grand or vernacular. The island of Burano, Venice, is famous for its houses painted in many different primary and pastel shades. Santorini's Greek Orthodox monastic domes are set against a black volcanic

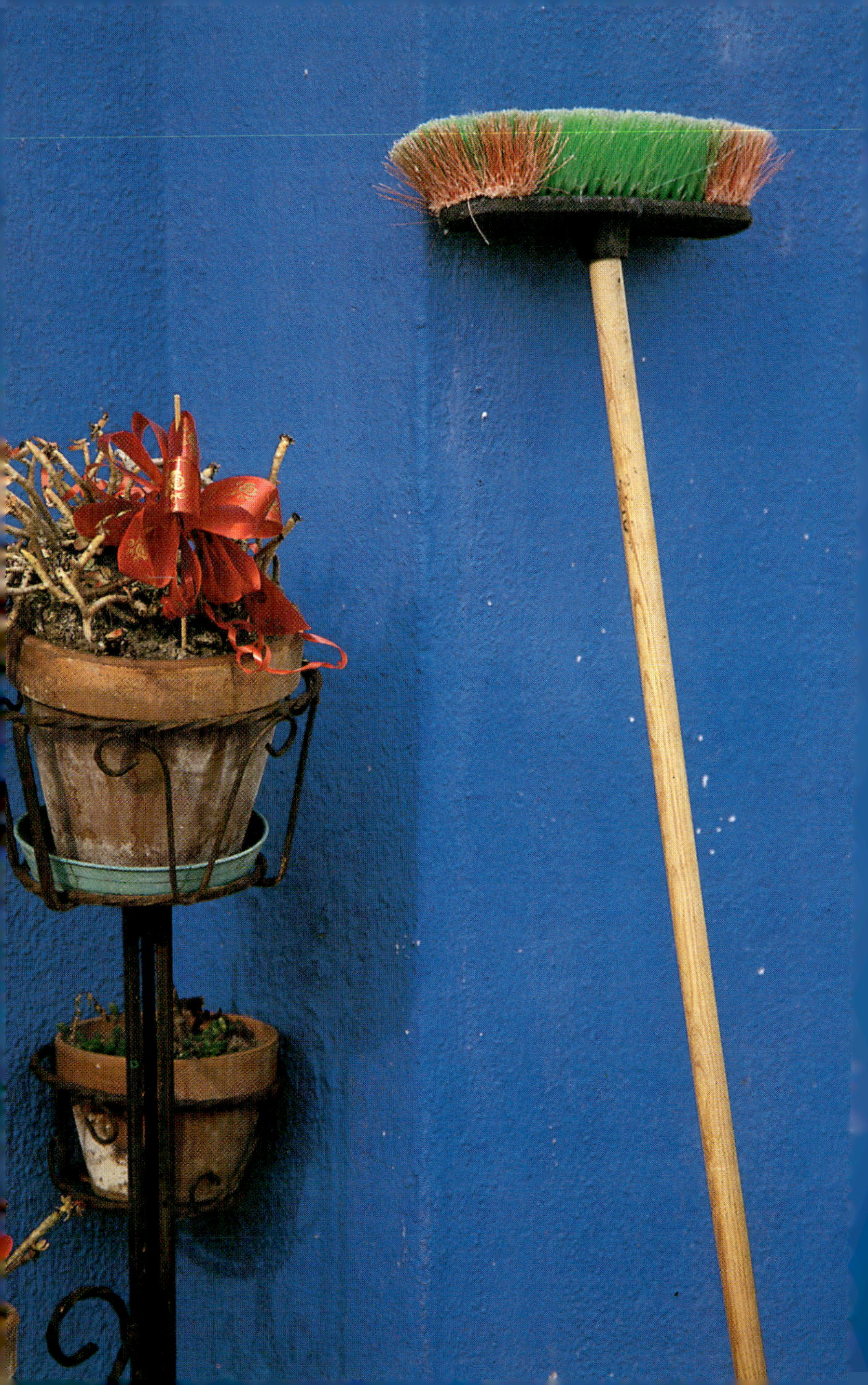

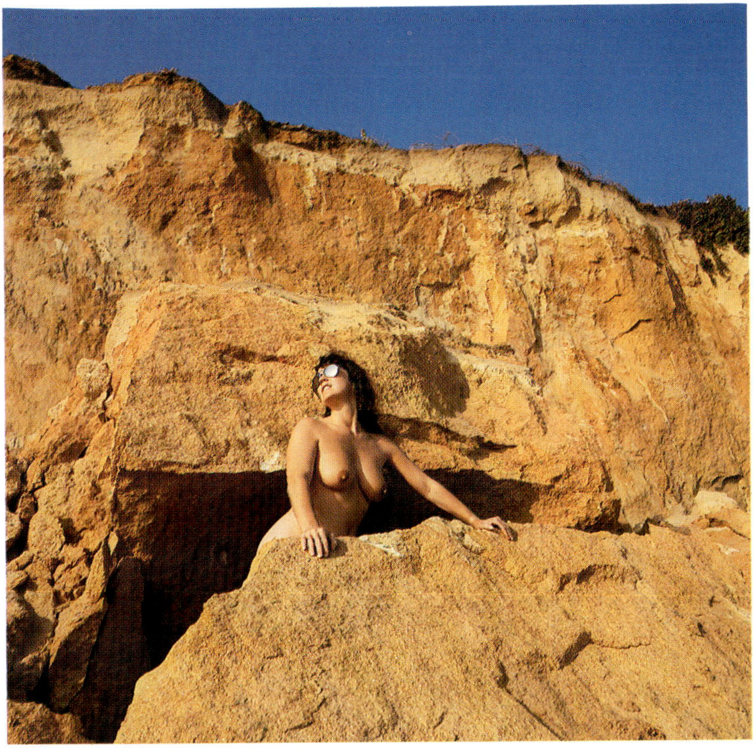

Left: the Venetian island of Burano is famous for its colourful houses, which make good close-ups. Above: sand and cliffs turn to vivid orange by sunset light on the Algarve coast near Quarteira, making a dramatic setting for a 'glamour' style shot on a beach where there is no problem with topless sunbathing.

landscape. Granada has its Alhambra, Barcelona its sculpture park and surrealist overtones, Tunisia its superb mosque at Kairouan, Athens its Acropolis. There are many more examples in every country and the guide books give a good idea of the potential.

Quality of light

Don't assume that bright light is 'harsh'. When the ground is light in colour and most buildings are whitewashed, the contrast is in fact low. Large areas of shadow can be included in pictures without becoming completely black. Taking pictures on the shady side of the street, you will find that colours take on a luminous quality and skin tones look particularly good. The light reflected off white walls forms the perfect outdoor 'studio lighting'.

Early and late in the day the colours are warmer, and low sun reveals texture. White walls help show the yellow or pink colour of sunset light. You can capture shadows and silhouettes effectively. Colours like blue or pale green can be degraded by evening light, but sand and sandstone cliffs or buildings are boosted in colour most effectively – beaches look great at sunset.

Colours

Impressions of faded colour are normally the result of over-exposed pictures or the overpowering effect of white and sandy tones in a shot. If you want to bring out the colours of clothing, ceramics, paint or foods put them against a contrasting or darker background. The colours will seem better by reflected, diffused light. Photographs taken in strong sunshine do not look any brighter.

Close-ups show colour better than distant views, so use a standard or long focus lens rather than a wide-angle. One exception is the colour of the sky; it gets darker towards the zenith, and wide-angle lenses emphasize its deep blue if you angle the camera upwards. Given a brightly coloured and contrasting subject this can be most effective.

A polarizing filter can help bring out colours. Avoid over-use! Unlike the green landscapes of countries with wetter climates, Mediterranean scenes do not have a wealth of foliage colour to be revealed and the sky needs no further enhancement. A polarizer can make the scene overpowering and dark.

People and customs

In the European Mediterranean most people are used to tourists and photographers. Remember that they are just like you. A village house near Positano probably costs as much as a detached house in an English suburb. You may think you are photographing a country smallholder when you're actually confronting the local magistrate who happens to be a keen gardener. It helps to say hello (in any language) and ask if you can take some pictures.

In the Eastern and North African Mediterranean matters are not very different, but the cultural gap is wider. You probably feel less trusting towards people with no good reason. The first thing to do is to adopt exactly the same approach as you would to a Frenchman or Italian. The Arab *bernous* looks like an old blanket but it frequently hides a city suit!

In general, avoid photo-

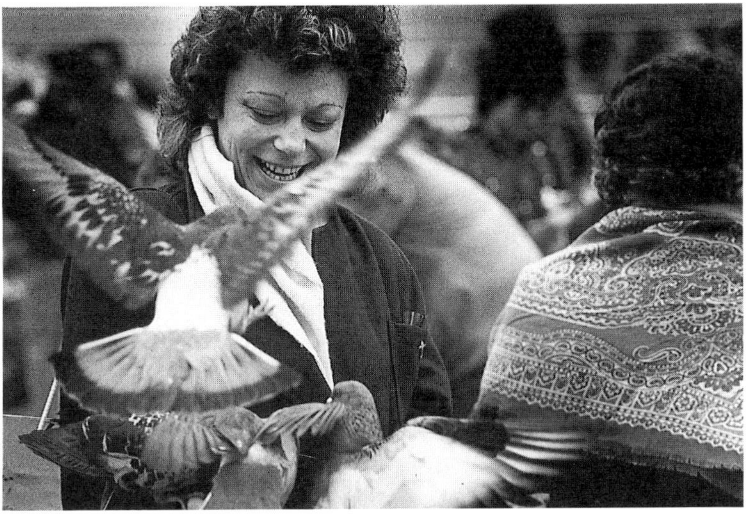

Tourist events make photographing people much easier. In public places, everyone expects to be photographed during the tourist season, so look out for candid shots. Language problems disappear!

graphing women and girls in Moslem countries and do not point your camera persistently at anyone who objects. Craftsmen, traders, entertainers and casual beggars should only be given the smallest coins in exchange for allowing a picture to be taken. Never accept an offer of an 'experienced guide' in places like Sousse or Marrakech as you will inevitably pay far more to be taken back to your hotel afterwards than the small sum asked for a tour of the souk!

A genuine guide can help by smooth the way to photograph local people, or stop you photographing anyone aggressive.

Special events

Occasionally you will find a very expensive period during the low season. This can be due to commercial activity or festivals. The Venice Carnival, with a movable date, provides a week in February or March when hotel accommodation is expensive and Venice is seriously overcrowded. It is also one of the most photogenic events in Europe. The Easter parades (Semana Santa) in Spain, the wine harvest in many countries, the arts festival in Arles, Christmas in Jerusalem – these are all popular trips.

Most publicity events are

widely photographed in guide books. It can help to read some up-to-date pictorial guides on your chosen area before booking, finding out the dates of major religious festivals, arts events and so on. The tourist office of the country involved will nearly always supply the next year's dates on request.

Avoid straightforward high season holiday periods which happen to coincide with national factory holidays. You pay more simply because there is more demand, and everywhere will be crowded. A good travel agent should be able to warn you about national holidays if asked.

Tackling problems

During a Mediterranean holiday, you may encounter a few technical problems. The first will be contrast – or at least judging it. In some areas very high buildings and narrow streets, without the benefit of whitewash, produce dense shadows combined with brilliant sun. The secret is to make sure you never include BOTH in the same shot.

Exposure metering systems can be fooled by large areas of light sand, sea, plain sky or white walls. With colour negative films, simply set the ISO rating to half the recommended setting if you can, or switch your backlight control on permanently. With slide films, allow one stop extra exposure on all shots which are predominantly white in content, half a stop extra on beach and sea scenes with plain (white or misty) skies.

Aerial haze, responsible for these colourless skies, can be cut to a slight extent with a polarizer. It can NOT be reduced by using so-called Haze filters. These protect your lens from damage, and reduce ultra-violet distance haze. Mediterranean haze is usually a slight mist, not UV. Generally it is better to avoid distant land or seascapes under these conditions; concentrate on close-up shots instead. Restricting your photography to early morning and late afternoon or evening will help.

Where to stay?

How you holiday has a big effect on your pictures. If the photography is an important part of your holiday, think hard about how you travel and where you stay.

Single-centre hotel accommodation is the cheapest form of package tour; off the plane, transfer to the hotel, stay there for a week or two, back to the airport. If you prefer this type of holiday pick your hotel carefully. One with extensive grounds, close to fields or a market, can provide plenty of subject-matter during short strolls with the camera before meals. One with nothing but other hotels and a beach offers little.

Car hire is a ready solution to single-centre hotel restrictions. On islands like Menorca or Rhodes a car gives you access to all points within a couple of days of leisurely driving. You don't need to hire the car every day. Even better solutions, for the enthusiast, include bicycle hire and using public transport. Both give you access to many more picture situations.

Multi-centre holidays

Two-centre and multi-centre tours are increasingly popular. You can find packages offering a week in Rome followed by a week at Lake Como, or mini-cruises from the Aegean to Egypt via Israel. For photography, the more ground you cover the better, but make sure that you are not on a schedule which prevents you from taking pictures!

Some tours are specially designed for photographers and stop for long enough at every location, even when on the move.

The most exciting forms of multi-centre holiday are the guest-house based tours which can be booked through the French, Spanish and other national agencies. The *paradores* network of country hotels and guest-houses in Spain could have been designed for photographers; a few days in a castle here, travel to a monastery in the mountains for a few more, then to a converted palace in a city – by car or rail, under your own steam or all previously booked.

Camping or caravanning offer similar contact with the countryside on a daily level, plenty of variety, and the ability to escape areas of bad weather. Static caravans, chalets and tents are less appealing to photographers, but some developments advertise specifically photographic seasonal packages. One villa complex in the South of France attracts many photographers just for the spring flowers each year.

Security is a major problem whenever you travel with camera equipment. Sadly, you are just as likely to have equipment stolen in a hotel as on a campsite, and the best solution is to keep your photo kit and wallet with you all the time. Never leave it in a tent, a hotel room, a car or a caravan. We have been 'lucky' over many years by doing exactly this. We have never had equipment stolen, but it has been with us 24 hours a day.

If you must leave things behind, even for a short period, be careful in your actions; do not be seen placing a large camera bag in the boot of a hire car and walking away. See if your hotel has a safe-deposit box; not all tourist hotels offer this, but if not the proprietor may be willing to look after valuables personally.

7: EXOTIC DESTINATIONS

UNFAMILIAR faces, dress and architecture bring fresh enthusiasm for photography. In very picturesque or unusual settings, small details are overlooked because the impact of the rest of the scene is so great. The Far East in general is now a modern and industrialized area, from India to Japan, and the smallest villages have power lines and advertising billboards. For the tourist with a camera these small Western intrusions don't matter very much – and there are still many special tourist developments and historic sites maintained in a photographically perfect state.

The Far East ranges from temperate to tropical in climate, and the most popular destinations are sub-tropical. Not many holidaymakers want to visit rain forests, but on the other hand developments like Thailand's Pattaya Beach are able to cope with tourism on a scale similar to the major European resorts.

Other general areas which have similar advantages and problems include islands such as Mauritius, the Seychelles, the Caribbean, Tahiti and new African beach resorts which have more in common with places like Pattaya than they do with safaris and tribal dances. It's worth considering all these areas together.

The photographic advantages have more to do with unfamiliarity than genuine pictorial merit. The first time you see the shape of a palm tree leaning out over a beach, you will photograph it; eventually you will ignore it, because the scene becomes familiar. You can find it in hundreds of different places.

People and customs do not become familiar in the same way. The very different facial expressions and manners of superficially similar people in Thailand, Hong Kong and Japan become more apparent with familiarity, and more interesting. The first-time tourist sees the Asiatic face with no distinction between Chinese and Japanese. It takes only a few days to know the difference immediately – and the same applies to races throughout the world.

As the instant appeal of a new place wears off your pictures will improve. Instead of photographing every shop or house, every group of bystanders, every market stall, you will look for the best.

Great variety

Exotic destinations are so varied that they cannot be discussed in detail. Seasonal variations are enormous and you should check carefully to ensure that your trip is at the right time. There are seasons of the year where the simple business of transfers to and from Bangkok airport is rendered totally uncertain. Sub-tropical areas have a much more reliable

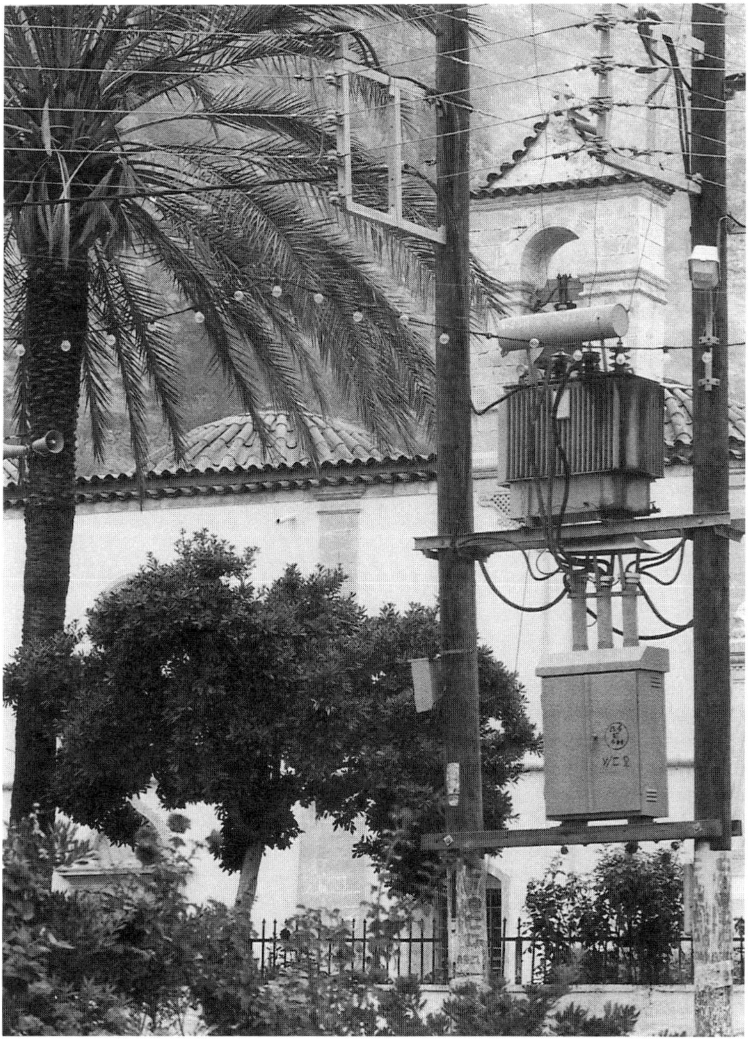

Distant places look picturesque – but in fact the cars, electricity cables and general untidiness would make them look commonplace to a local. It is the unexpected which adds to the shot for the visitor.

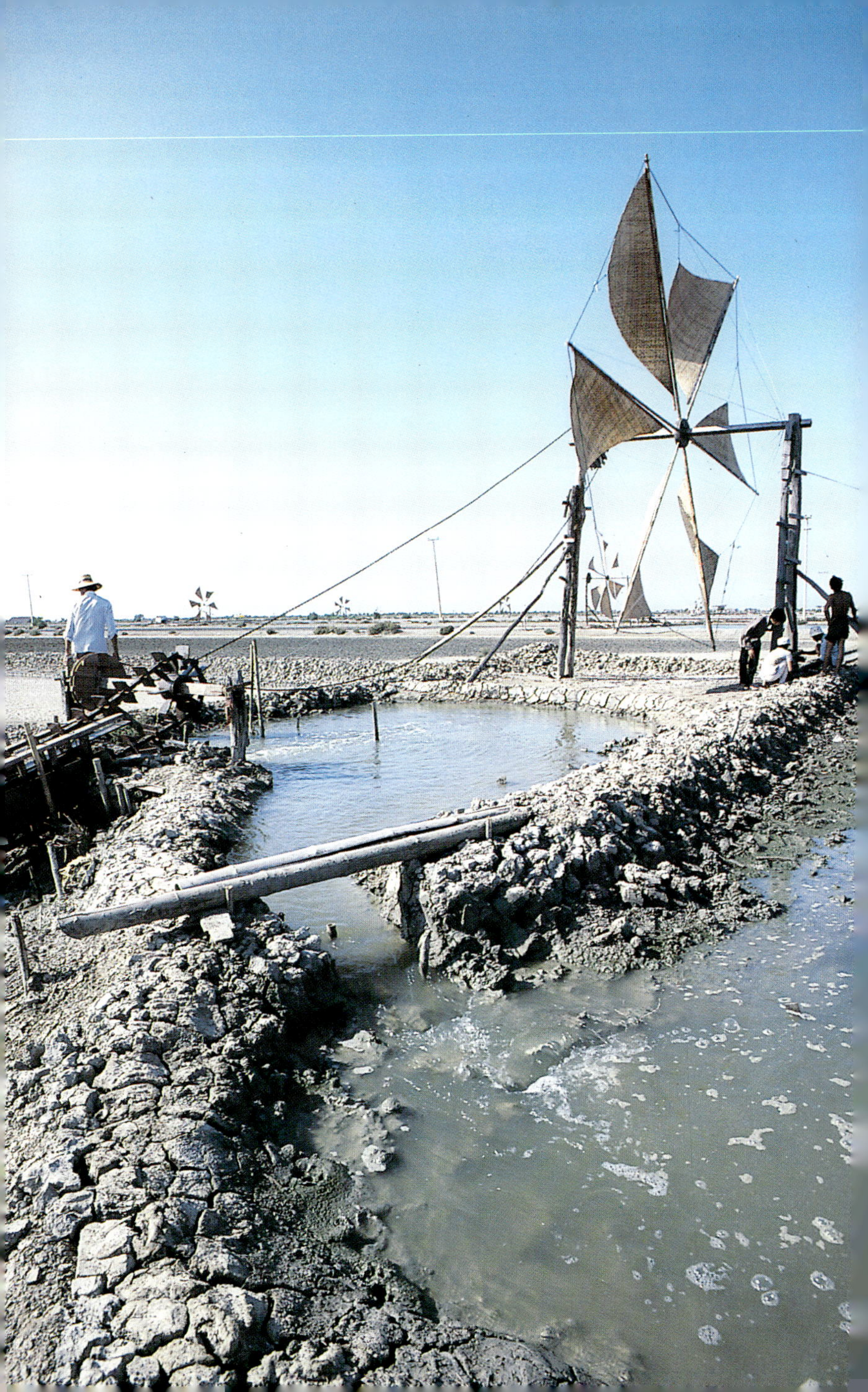

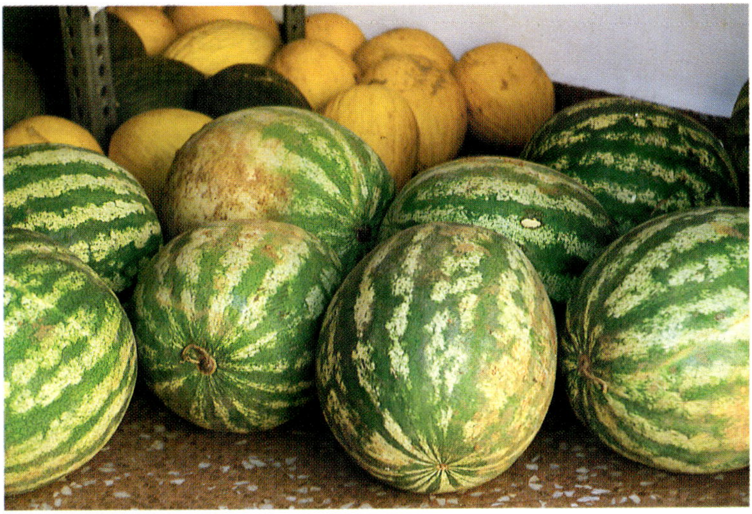

Left: finding genuinely strong pictorial subjects, like these Thai salt-pan windpumps seen through a 20mm wide-angle, makes better pictures easy. Above: look for close-ups when the overall scene disappoints.

and rigid annual cycle of weather than temperate areas. A good travel company will tell you precisely which weeks of the year will be accompanied by gales and thunderstorms, and which month will have the best flowers.

Suffice to say that the WRONG timing may be disastrous for photography and holiday activities alike. In many cases there are no tours available to some destinations at certain times of year. Making your own stop-over arrangements during these periods is a risky business.

Companies like Kuoni which specialize in exotic locations avoid 'bad weeks' successfully.

Local colour

To use the phrase in an alternative sense, local colour has a considerable influence on pictures. From Burma eastwards the Far East has one advantage; the people are light-skinned, and even when a face is shaded by a wide-brimmed coolie hat your picture will show some detail. In parts of India, most of Africa, the Caribbean and islands like the Seychelles skin colour can range from deep brown to an almost blue-black.

The results can be seen in holiday photographs everywhere; people, even when photographed close-up, become nothing but black featureless cut-outs against a brilliantly lit background. You are very strongly advised to use a camera with a spot metering function, or even to use fill-in flash. In bright tropical sunshine, most locals will sit with their eyes shaded or their backs to the sun. Attempts to shoot this kind of situation with a compact AF camera are next to useless unless you have the facility to switch the flash on as well.

The colours of buildings, streets, animals and all kinds of other things have a great influence on the success or otherwise of your pictures. Dark brown wood or mud buildings can look very flat and uninteresting. A similar construction in a bleached timber or with a straw-coloured reed thatch will make a far better picture.

The best areas for photography are those where paint is used to decorate houses (the Caribbean, for example). Places like Jaipur in India, where the local stone has a beautiful natural rose-pink hue, come a close second. Sometimes the apparent attractions of a place do not translate well into pictures. The klongs of Bangkok, with their timber houses rising from the canal on stilts, rarely photograph well from the boat trips. The house interiors are dark, domestic accoutrements are very suburban and range from piles of pots and pans to full washing lines, the water is a filthy colour most of the year and the moored boats are likely to be modern motor launches. Yet this is the one aspect of Bangkok which every visitor wants to photograph!

Architecture

In sub-tropical areas, unlike the Mediterranean, the architecture often has more in common with rainy northern places. The roofs are pitched to throw off heavy seasonal rains and have deep eaves to provide shade and keeping the splashing water from soaking the walls.

While these features are picturesque, they cause problems. The roof becomes the dominant part of the building and you have to stand well back to get the best views; a wide-angle lens does no good, as from a close viewpoint you cannot see the roof itself. The overhanging eaves cast shadows, and people prefer to sit in the shade.

City architecture is rarely like this, though arcades and covered areas replace the shade of the eaves. City architecture is becoming so universal in its appearance that there is little point in photographing it anywhere unless it is dramatic. The view of Hong Kong from the top of the funicular railway is a classic example, and a good reason for buying a 20mm wide-angle lens before (or during) a visit. Street-level views of Hong Kong are often unsatisfactory.

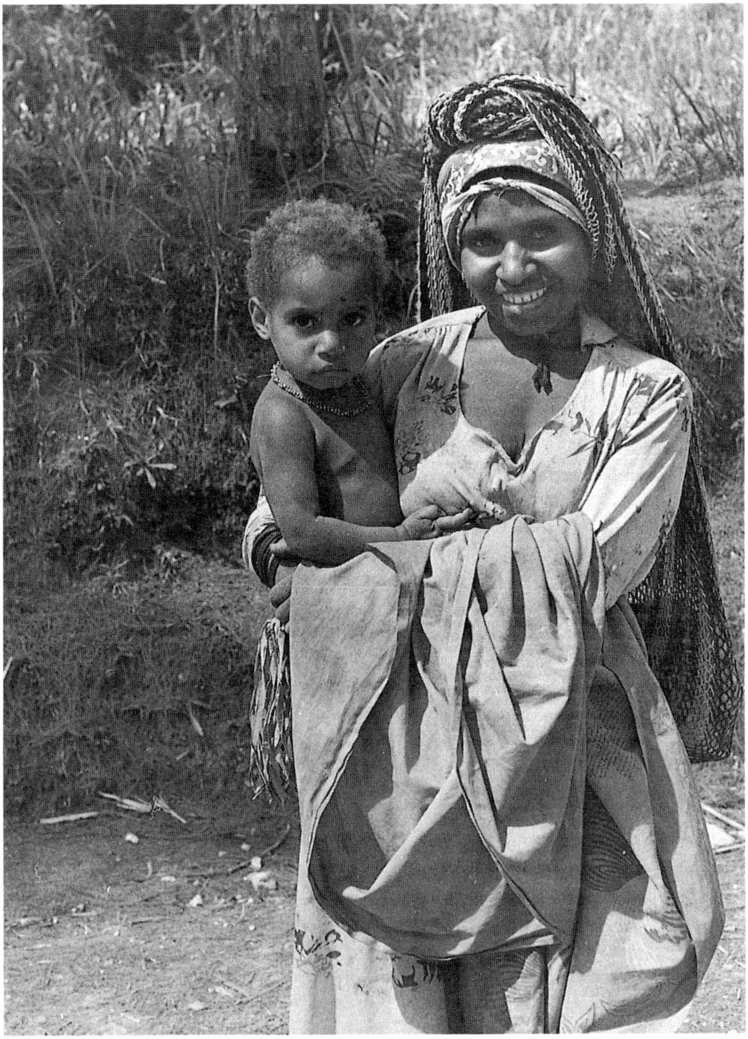

This portrait, taken by Robert Motz, shows how dark skin tones can be rendered correctly. Pick a neutral background, not in brilliant sun, and make sure the face is not in shade itself. Careful printing helps here.

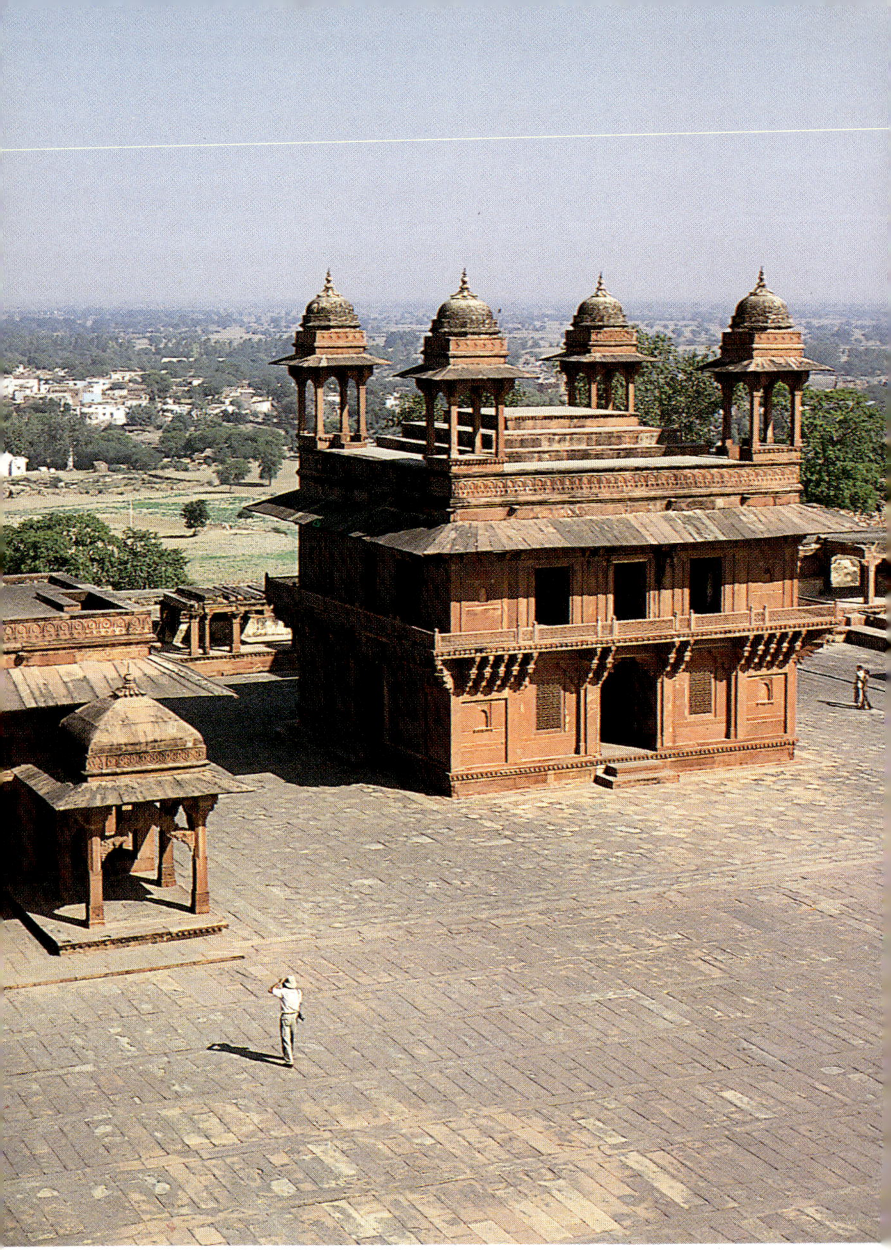

Light from directly overhead does not detract from the colour, texture or modelling of the ancient buildings of Fatehpur Sikri in this photograph. Lower light might have cast unwanted long shadows.

Light

Exotic destinations are selected for tropical heat. In the high season this means that the sun is almost overhead for the two hours either side of midday. This is the time when anyone sensible wears a hat, and any sensible hat casts a firm shadow over all the face; any sensible photographer puts the camera away, too.

Midday light does work for a few limited subjects. Courtyards in the centre of temples are fully lit at this time, and one or two walls will have the light skimming down them and revealing texture. The ground itself will be flatly lit, but your picture will probably not feature the ground. Mid-day light does no harm to a site like Fatehpur Sikri or the temples at Nara in Japan; if anything, it makes routine photography easier as there is no direction which becomes 'against the light' and causes lens-flare.

No doubt morning and evening light will reveal better pictures of individual parts of places like this, but in practice mid-day sun is not as bad as it's made out to be for general record photography.

The ends of the day provide much better opportunities for photographing people. For one thing, they are active; in the noonday sun your most likely subjects will indeed be English tourists, if not mad dogs. Morning and evening see ploughing in the fields, markets opening up, street vendors setting up stalls, ox carts trundling down rough roads, and people with their faces properly lit by the low sun.

People and customs

So varied are your potential destinations on an exotic trip that comments on local customs become meaningless. The attitude of the Balinese to photography is not the same as that of the Thailander; your experiences in a small Indian village may not be echoed in New Delhi. Greater distances create greater differences.

On the whole, it is reasonable to assume that people who place themselves in a tourist location will not object to photography. Throughout the Buddhist world, temples are meeting-places where people eat and trade. The temple becomes more of a market-place, and you can photograph people freely. Even inside many shrines the camera is welcome.

Moslem worshippers would not welcome this approach. You can not take photographs inside the Taj Mahal and should not try. Outside, even the local people you see are probably day-trippers and the real locals are the ones who try to secure a small tip by showing you the best viewpoint (the one used in the postcards!).

The same applies to public places generally. Those markets which attract coach-trips of

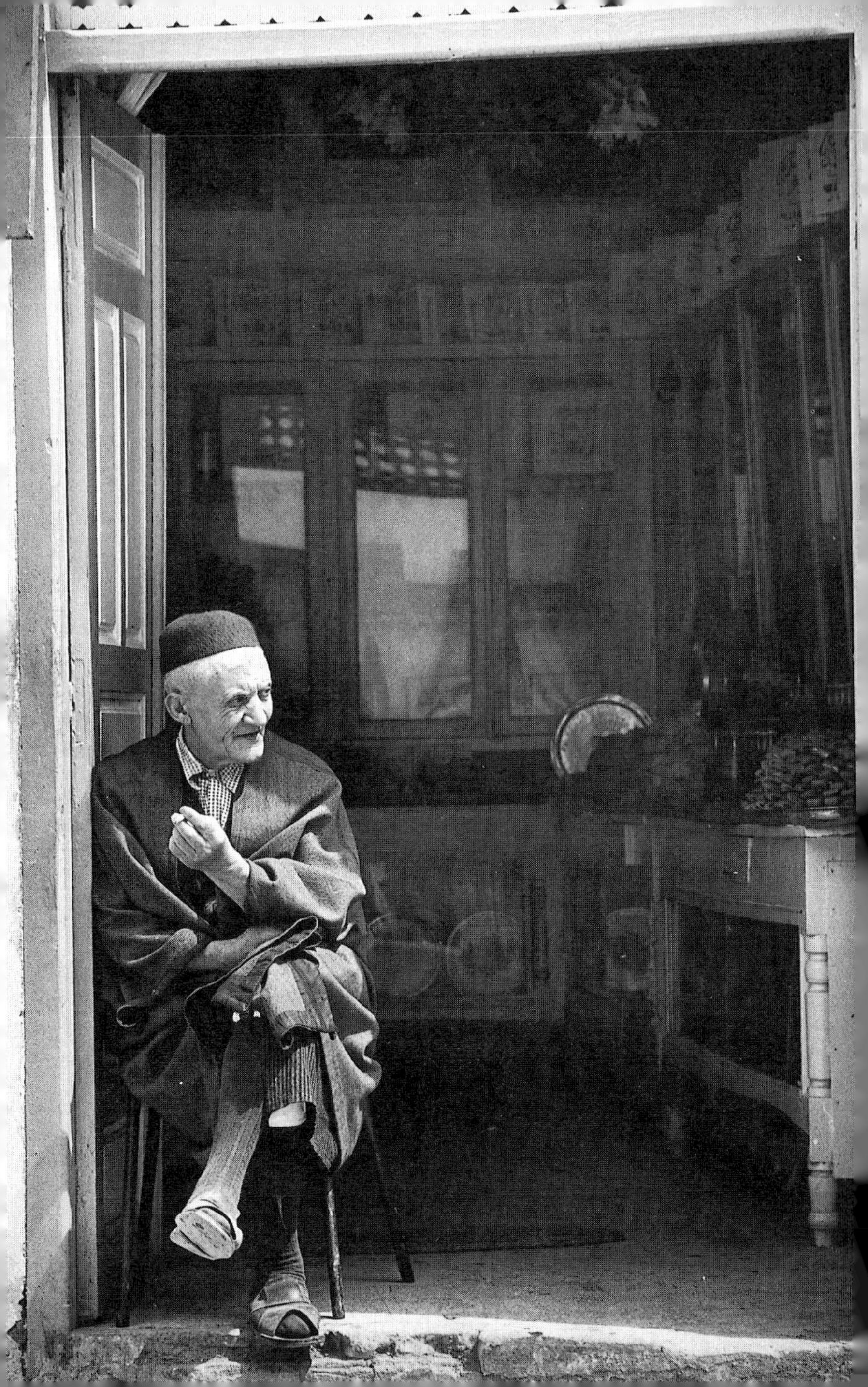

tourists are used to photography; every stall-holder will be photographed hundreds of times each day, and some get to know that they are photogenic and dress up to aid the effect. Village streets off the beaten track may have similar stalls and people but probably never see a tourist. Sometimes the result is charming friendliness and courtesy regardless of language barriers; in other places it can be the reverse. You have to judge for yourself.

Problems

Sub-tropical destinations suffer from problems we have already looked at; high humidity, overhead light at mid-day, and dust or haze at some times of year. The solutions are much the same as in any area, but particular attention should be paid to the combination of heat and humidity, and the dust as opposed to haze.

It is very important never to leave a cool air-conditioned hotel with your camera open and ready for use if the humidity is very high. Video cameras often have a special dew-point warning light to show when condensation may be forming, but still cameras have never featured this. Your first warning will be a camera which feels wet to the hands and has an eyepiece or viewfinder obscured by condensation.

At this stage is is VITAL that you do not remove the lens, open the camera back to load a film, or remove a filter, lens cap or any other part of the camera. You must simply wait until the entire camera has warmed up thoroughly, even if this means sitting down and putting it on a table in the sun. Remove any cold items from your camera case and place these in the sun too, to warm up. Don't place your films in the sun!

Some people refrigerate their holiday films, because modern colour films give better results if they are kept below 55°F. Be very careful not to remove a cold film from your hotel room's fridge, take it outdoors into humid air, and immediately unwrap it and load it. The film may be ruined. Let it warm up for two hours before use, and keep a couple of un-refrigerated films ready. After exposure, seal the film in its plastic canister and refrigerate whenever you can. The colours will be better if you keep the films cool and do not let them reach a temperature over 75°F after exposure. Amateur films like Kodachrome are more tolerant of temperature changes than professional films like Ektachrome EPR 64.

In tourist areas, you can expect to be able to photograph almost anyone in public (left). Do not assume that the attitudes will be the same in a small village.

Places and events

One of the best ways to enjoy your photography is to plan your visits, especially to far-away places. Just as a visitor to Spain will find Easter interesting, a visitor to Brazil will be considerably rewarded by timing things to see the Carnival.

Religious and social events can be superb for photography. The Festival of Lights in Bangkok involves the launching of thousands of candles onto the city's lakes (not the canals, as the litter produced was considered offensive by the government) with fireworks in the streets. In Japan, there is a week in November when the parklands around the shrines are in full autumn colours and parents bring very young children in full traditional dress for a ceremony.

On Far Eastern tours in particular you may find the recommended itinerary is full of temple visits. It is hard to visit any Buddhist country without seeing one temple a day. From the photographer's point of view one Golden Buddha is much like the next. Look for off-beat trips; you can be shown into the traditional home of a Japanese family, walk across salt-pans, be ferried by rickshaw round a nature reserve, see displays of the martial arts, look round a farm – all kinds of options are available in addition to the straightforward scenic and cultural tours.

Activities don't always mix with photography. You may be able to hire a boat and catch something unusual in the Seychelles, but don't take a full SLR outfit with you. If you plan to do this kind of thing, make sure you have the right kind of compact, weatherproof camera. The keen photographer may be better off taking the trip without a camera and waiting for local fishermen to land their own catches and photograph them on shore.

Security

Returning to the subject of security, be very careful on any multi-centre tour as opposed to a single destination package. Despite increasing standards of honesty and efficiency at airports worldwide, luggage is systematically opened in many airports, presumably by organized gangs. If it is known that you will catching connecting flights or making single-day stopovers, you run a much greater risk than people staying for several days who are able to lay their complaints fully.

Airlines offering intercontinental flights have a comprehensive scale of compensation which you should enquire about immediately any loss occurs. Within hours you will be issued with sufficient (dollar) credit to allow you to purchase a basic wardrobe and travelling essentials – but not to replace your cameras or film!

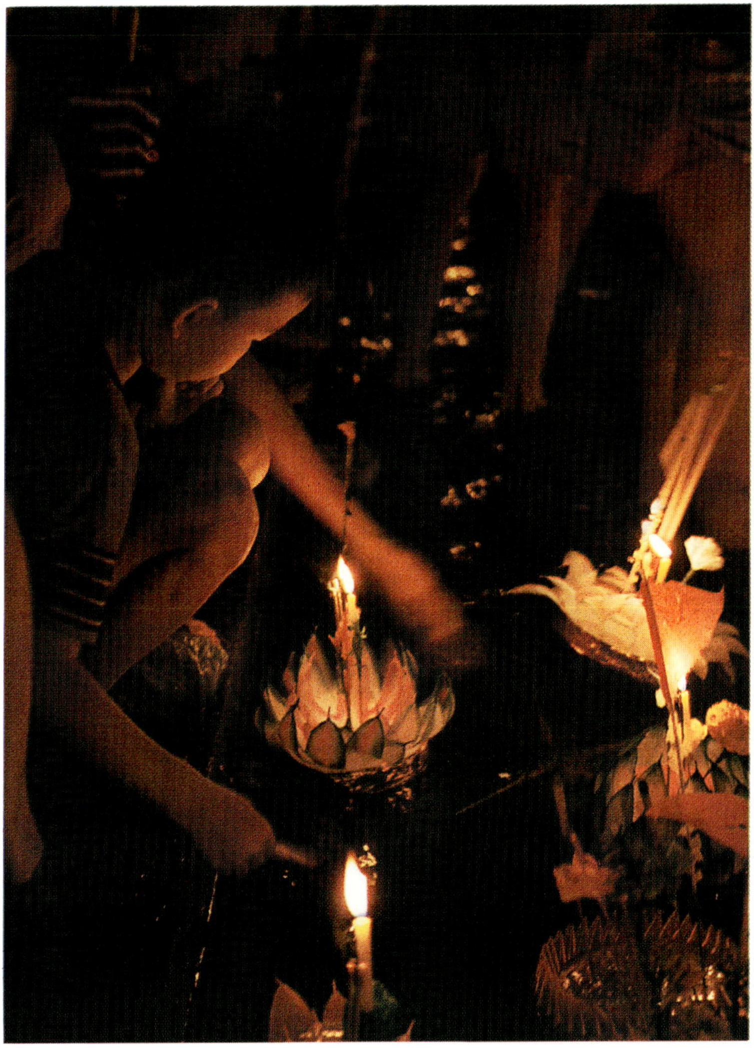

The Festival of Lights in Bangkok happens once a year, and it is difficult to photograph even with a special fast ISO 1000 film, as used here. It is worth seeing this November festival with or without a camera.

8: FURTHER AFIELD

SPECIAL interest and activity holidays are often planned with photography in mind. If you decide to travel overland through Nepal or take a game reserve safari tour to Kenya, you will not be alone with your camera. Many people are not keen photographers, but keen on some other aspect of the trip – the wildlife, the archaeology, mountaineering, or pure adventure.

Whether photography is your main objective or a means to record an experience which you will be unlikely to repeat every year, you should end up with exceptional subjects. How can you be sure of turning these into exceptional pictures, given the difficulties involved?

Specialist photo-tours can be a great help. For every overland trip through Nepal organized by a purely travel and exploration orientated company, you can find a similar trip accompanied by an expert photographer. For many years the Himalayan mountaineer Alfred Gregory has accompanied such expeditions, as has the ornithologist David Oswin – both expert photographers. No doubt each year will bring new expert tour-leaders into the field. The photographic magazines carry advertising for trips like this, and some tour operators have a special section on interest and activity holidays which includes photography.

On an accompanied photo trip, you may have access to knowledge and experience (the tour leader), ideas and advice (your companions on the trip) and equipment (sponsored or supplied by a camera company, or borrowed on a mutual basis from companions using similar camera systems). You cannot expect these from a regular trip.

Secondly, the photo trip will be scheduled to visit areas known for their photogenic qualities, at the right time, with specific stops planned. There will be no rushing past spectacular sunsets; everyone will wait for the crowds from the last coach-load to leave; your fellow tourists will not get in your way. Moreover, one person will often carry a single tripod to be shared by the whole group – an important thing when you don't want to be weighed down.

Progress through customs is likely to be easier when a party can be identified as a purely photographic one. The tour leader will probably be able to gather up all your films and pass them through for a hand search instead of X-raying. In short, there are many advantages in joining a mainly photographic trip when venturing further afield. The destinations range from Greenland to the Himalayas, up the Amazon or to the forests of Borneo – at an appropriate cost.

Ordinary (non-photographic) special interest holidays are equally wide-ranging, but you are able to find many at a lower cost.

THE ADVANTAGE OF PHOTO TRIPS

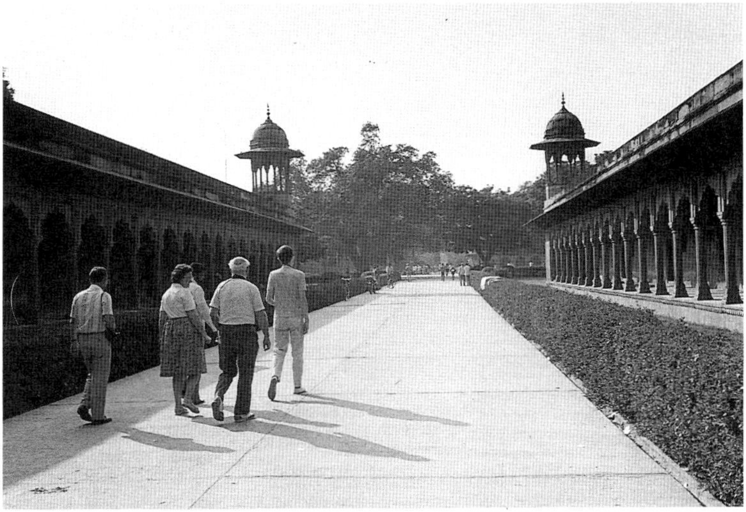

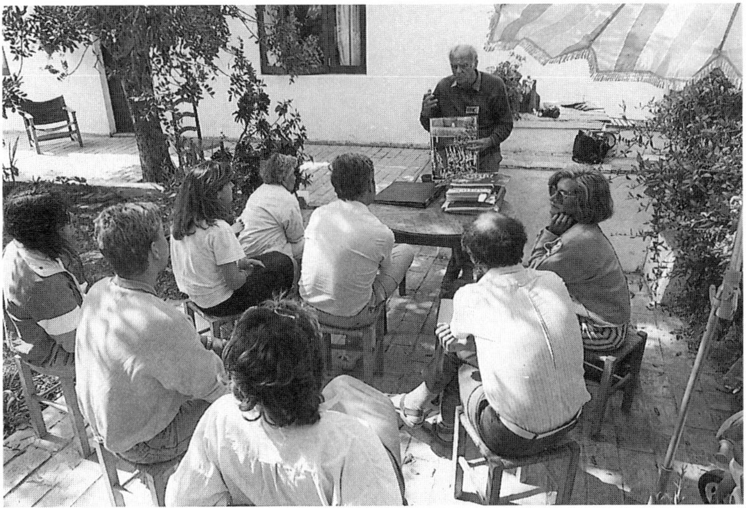

Photographic tours have their advantages in exotic destinations. A group of amateur photographers visits the Taj Mahal (top) and a more serious party (below) discusses photography with lecturer Peter Johns.

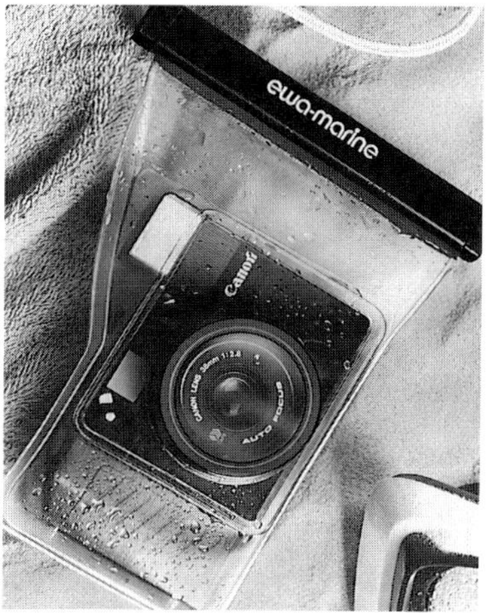

Getting into the water with your camera can be a risky business, unless you have a waterproof or splashproof model. The Ewa-Marin camera housing, above, holds most compact AF cameras and can be used underwater to normal snorkelling depths. The Konica Jump, below, is a splashproof camera which can not be submerged. The external sealing on cameras like this makes them ideal for all kinds of outdoor activity as well as on the beach.

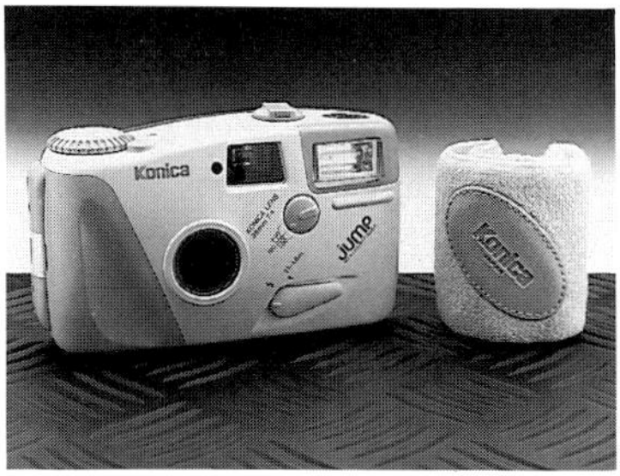

There is no need to go half way across the world to ride horses across marshland and see flamingos at sunset. You can do this in the French Camargue. At home, wherever that may be, you can probably find activity-based weekends, weeks or longer run from hotels, colleges during the summer vacation, or special field centres or sports complexes.

Sea, sand and surf

A traditional beach holiday can be combined with learning new skills and using your photography if you equip yourself for shooting on the shoreline. You have a wide choice of camera equipment ranging from simple sub-aqua snapshot cameras (at around the same price as a normal AF compact) to full underwater systems, or special housings to protect your normal camera.

The simplest and cheapest way to try underwater and in-the-water photography uses a flexible plastic bag called a Ewa-Marin housing. The camera is loaded with film, switched on and set to programmed or shutter priority exposure if possible, and placed inside the bag. The top is sealed with a pair of metal bars which prevent any water from entering. Welded-in flat glass plates of optical quality cover the lens and viewfinder areas. When immersed, the air trapped in the bag is enough to prevent the camera from being squashed by

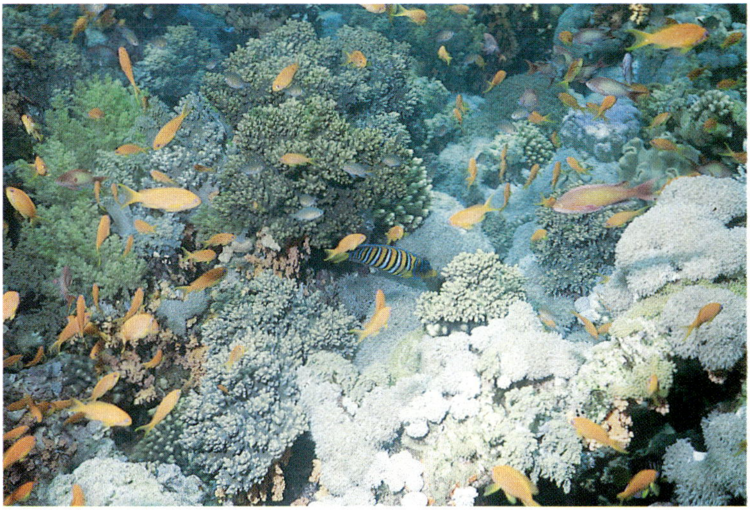

The undersea landscape is best captured on colour film in shallow sunlit waters at close distances. Deeper diving creates blue, murky pictures and colours are lost with distance. Photo: DIVER magazine.

water pressure and will allow it to float if 'lost' accidentally underwater. The glass plates are pressed into contact, and a kind of rubber glove which extends into the housing allows you to operate the camera controls.

The best kind of SLR to use with this housing is an autofocus, auto exposure model with a motor-wind and a camera-top flash. You may find it possible to operate a zoom satisfactorily inside the housing, though the space will restrict you to a 35-70mm type. In practice this is an ideal lens to use.

With your camera safe inside this simple marine protection, you can shoot watersports from close quarters, swim up to get better shots of windsurfing, or you can make shallow dives when snorkeling. This type of housing is not strong enough to protect the camera from pressure at aqualung depths. In practice photography is much simpler in shallow clear waters, which often have plenty of colourful fish and plants, and the 3-5m diving limit imposed by simple flexible housings is no disadvantage.

Deeper sub-aqua photography calls for a simple underwater compact 35mm camera. These cost about as much as a low-price 35mm SLR and do not have any interchangeable lenses, just a built-in flash and a simple focusing system, with a large frame-finder for underwater viewing through a mask. They can also be used in boats and on the beach with the normal viewfinder also built-in. A typical underwater compact camera can go to at least 15 metres; at this depth, the flash is needed to obtain good colours, and the best shots are close-ups at around one metre distance.

To extend photography to the practical limits of aqualung diving, you need a proper rigid housing for a 35mm SLR, or the special Nikonos underwater camera with its interchangeable lenses and separate flash. The latter is probably the best choice, as the housings for SLRs are expensive and bulky. The Nikonos, available in various forms since the late 1950s, is a rugged all-purpose camera perfectly suitable for use on land as well.

The advantages of a special camera or housing on the beach are considerable. Instead of having to protect your camera from sand and water, you can run into the sea with it, photograph your family and children in and out of the water as well as under the water, and come back with some unusual and exciting pictures.

Don't forget that picking a resort with a real village or harbour enables you to get good local colour and atmosphere shots. Be up at dawn and photograph the fishermen bringing in their catch. Pick a west- or south-facing beach and you have the added benefit of sunsets over the sea or shoreline, and seascapes made livelier by the sun sparkling off the surface during the day. You do not get this with north-facing beaches at any time. Eastern coasts enjoy the sunrise, but will you be there to enjoy it at leisure? Part of the fun of photography on a beach holiday is sitting with a drink and a camera watching the sun sink and picking the right moments to take sunsets, with silhouetted figures on the beach or boats on the water.

If you do want to tackle underwater photography, buy a specialist book on the subject. It is not as simple as it seems – even the angle of view of a lens changes when you place the camera underwater – and you may be disappointed at your first attempts. The golden rule is to keep near the surface and take pictures when the sun is high.

When you surface, remember to wipe the glass lens-front, as any droplets remaining will ruin photographs taken on land – they cause small areas of blur, or bright patches where the sun catches the water. Keep a soft flannel to wipe the lens cover, and always rinse the camera in fresh water after taking it into the sea.

Winter sports

At the other end of the year, the winter sports holiday also offers great photographic opportunities. The main reason for FAILING to get good snow scenes and mountain landscapes is not being there. When it snows at home you probably stay inside by the fire, make a snowman in the garden and drive your car cautiously on main roads. During a winter sports holiday you get right into the snow-covered countryside, in just the type of hilly country you would never visit when roads are icy.

Snow scenes call for care in exposure. They are best with the sun out, regardless of the time of day. When most of the picture consists of snow you should allow one and a half *f*-stops in extra exposure. If the picture has plenty of houses, trees and people in it, one stop should be enough. If there is a very deep blue sky occupying more than half the shot, do not even bother to correct the exposure.

Bracket exposures and take several frames of the same view, at normal, plus half, plus one, and plus 1.5 stops exposure. If you have ISO 100 film in your camera, and the meter gave you a reading of 1/250 at *f*16, this would mean giving exposures of:

1/250 *f*16
1/250 *f*13 (11 – 16)
1/250 *f*11
1/250 *f*9.5 (8 – 11)

You can do this by setting the exposures manually, using a special bracketing facility if your camera offers this, using a factorial over-ride dial (0, +1/2, +1, +1.5), or re-setting the ISO film speed (ISO 100, 64, 50, 32). Cameras which offer a backlight control can be used for one shot without, and a further shot with this control in use.

Colour negative (print) film users should simply set the ISO film speed on the camera to HALF the recommended setting for the entire duration of any winter sports holiday. With an ISO 100 film, set your camera to ISO 50. You should only change this back when taking flash pictures inside in the evenings.

Mountains are hard to photograph and a few tips are useful. These are:

* Avoid wide-angle lenses
* Never look up from the bottom of a hill
* Find a viewpoint half-way up a hillside to get the best view of the opposite side of a valley
* Keep the amount of sky showing in the picture to a minimum

The most impressive mountain scenes are taken with long focus lenses, not wide-angles, and rarely feature the mountain the photographer is actually standing on. The 50mm standard lens is an excellent general lens for alpine landscapes. A polarizing filter should not be needed unless

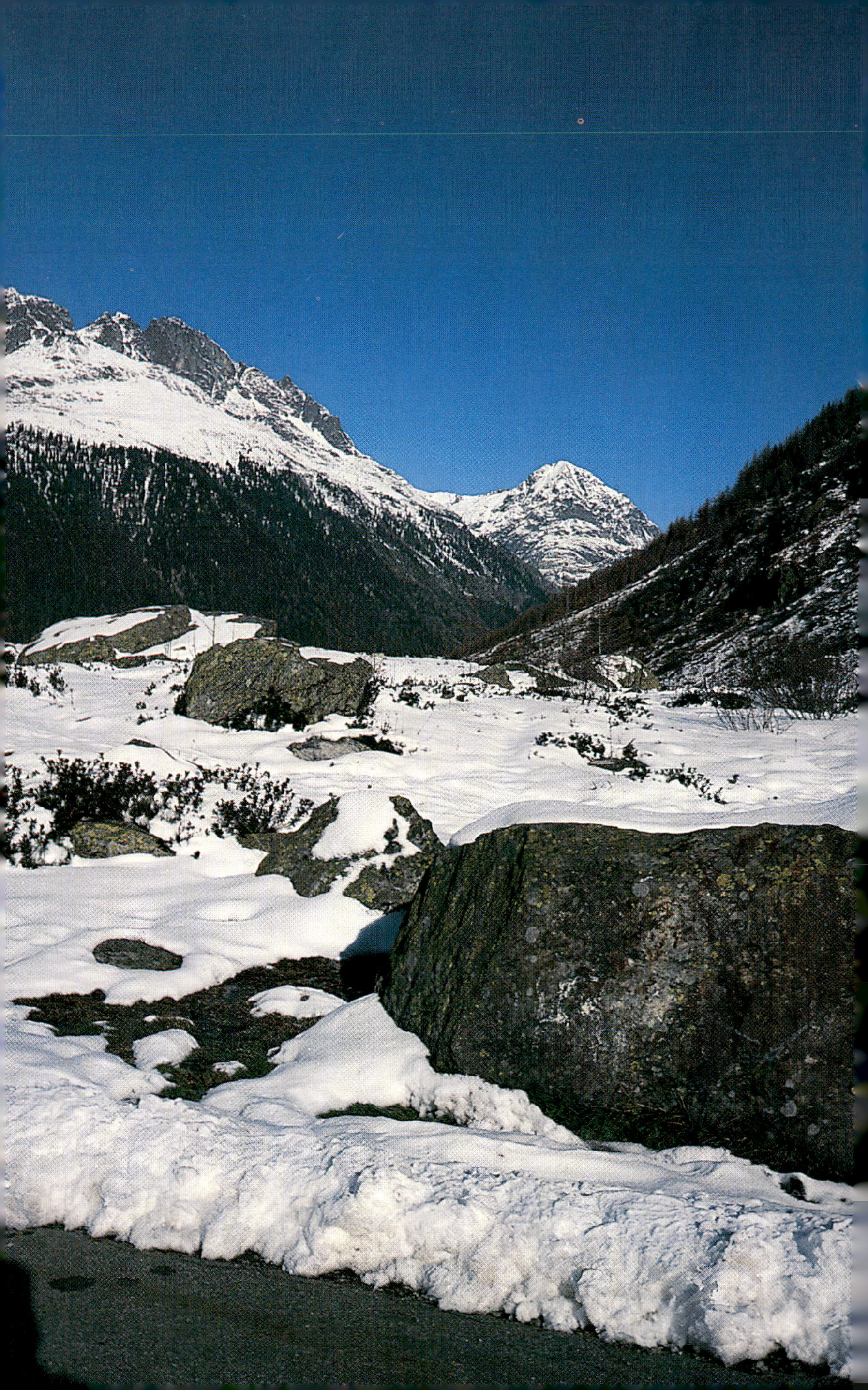

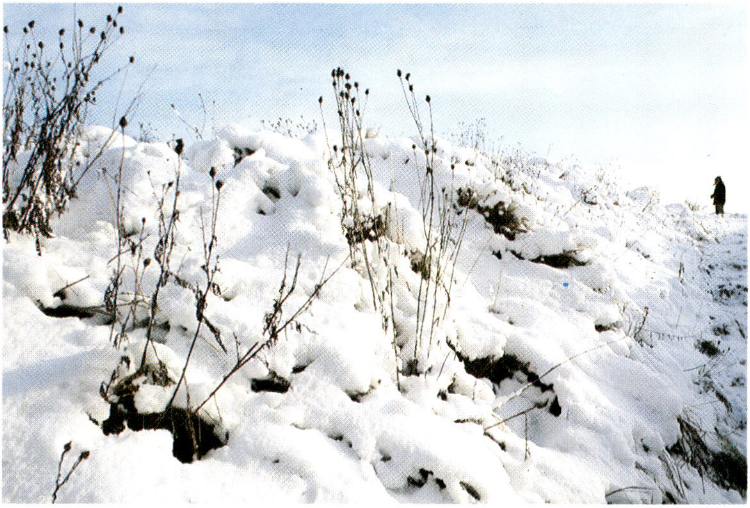

Above: a scene consisting mainly of snow will require one and a half stops extra exposure with most cameras. Left: a scene with a blue sky and more dark areas needs no correction – photo by Derek Grossmark.

you want deep blue-black skies.

Watch the performance of your batteries in cold weather; if possible, use a fresh set and keep the camera under your coat most of the time. You can buy a special battery pack on a remote cable to fit many cameras; keeping this next to your skin will improve the performance many times. Cold batteries are only one-fifth as efficient as batteries at room temperature.

Condensation will form if your camera is brought from cold outdoor conditions into a warm heated room, particularly if the atmosphere is humid. As with tropical humidity, the advice is to leave the camera alone, without removing any lenses or filters or opening the back to load film, until it has warmed up enough to evaporate the moisture.

Winter sports photography lends itself to action techniques with cameras using a fast flash speed of 1/250th, like synchro-sun flash. The secret of good winter sports action photography is to get the skier picked out against blue sky rather than white snow; any attempts to take panned shots against snow will fail badly, and the figure will seem ghosted or lose hands or feet. This is because the white snow burns through the blurred image of the skier.

Against a dark background such as an area of mountainside in shade or a polarized sky, the subject will stand out much better and the colours of ski outfits can be seen in their true brightness. Techniques like synchro-sun flash (for close-up shots only) and panning work well.

Off-beat holidays

Specialist travel firms offer holidays covering a vast scope of interests. Some of these are ideal for photography – others are not.

EASTERN BLOC tours taking in cities like Prague and Leningrad are fascinating for the student of art, architecture and history. You may find your photography limited by the programme and in some places it will be discouraged or forbidden. The pictures you do take may be even more interesting because relatively few photographers visit countries where photography is restricted.

ARCTIC CIRCLE and Icelandic trips, especially in midsummer when the sun never sets and the 'sunset' is very long and colourful, are superb for photography. It is vital to take a polarizing filter and a tripod, as well as a wide-angle lens of around 24mm to capture the sweeping sky and sea views. A good telephoto lens around 300mm is useful for photographing birds.

THIRD WORLD countries are most likely to be visited in a context of voluntary service or working holidays. A basic outfit, preferably mechanical, should be backed up with a pocketable compact camera and an instant-picture camera if you can afford to take a few packs of Polaroid film. Relationships with people are important during this kind of visit and instant prints are greatly appreciated.

GEOLOGICAL, ecological and wildlife trips visit places like the Galapagos Islands which are of scientific and popular interest. Take plenty of film and batteries, and do not expect to be able to obtain anything when in a remote area. If you are going on this kind of trip you should already be experienced enough in all aspects to get things right – if not, you are unlikely to benefit from the trip itself.

FESTIVALS and fairs like the Munich Oktoberfest or New Orleans Mardi Gras offer a wealth of subjects to the photographer. Keep your equipment light, using just two or three lenses; make sure you have a compact AF camera, and a good flashgun, as so much takes place after dark or indoors. If you want to join in, the compact is unobtrusive... everyone else has one, too.

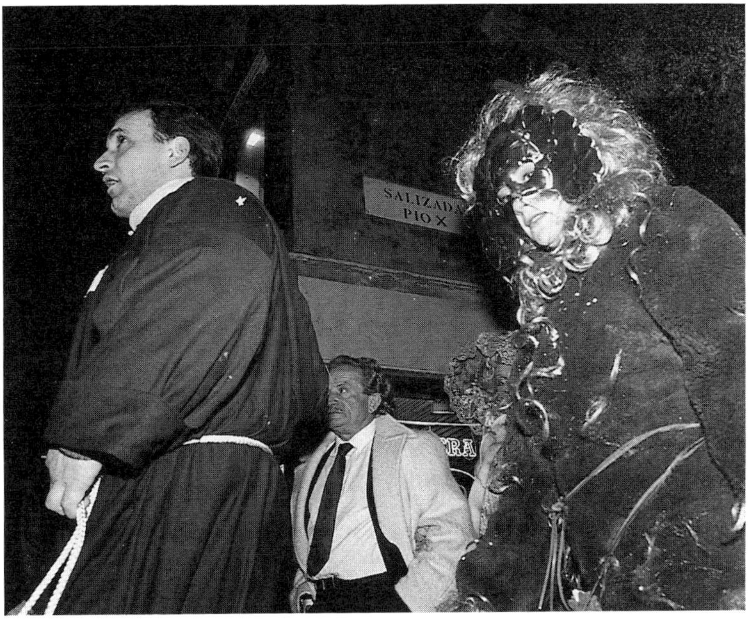

So much action at events like beer festivals takes place after dark that a flashgun becomes essential. Look for characters and 'set pieces' which are more often than not intended for the camera.

SPORTS events do not give much scope for photography unless you have the appropriate passes or seats available. Olympic and similar stadium events call for a very long telephoto lens (300mm to 600mm) and a tripod. Often the seating does not allow this. Floodlit sports events need special film or colour filters and are very hard to capture well. The major exceptions to the disappointment of photographers at sports events are large-scale rallies and races – hot air balloons, yachts, road rallies, river boat races and so on. With time to study the routes you can secure a good viewpoint and take better pictures.

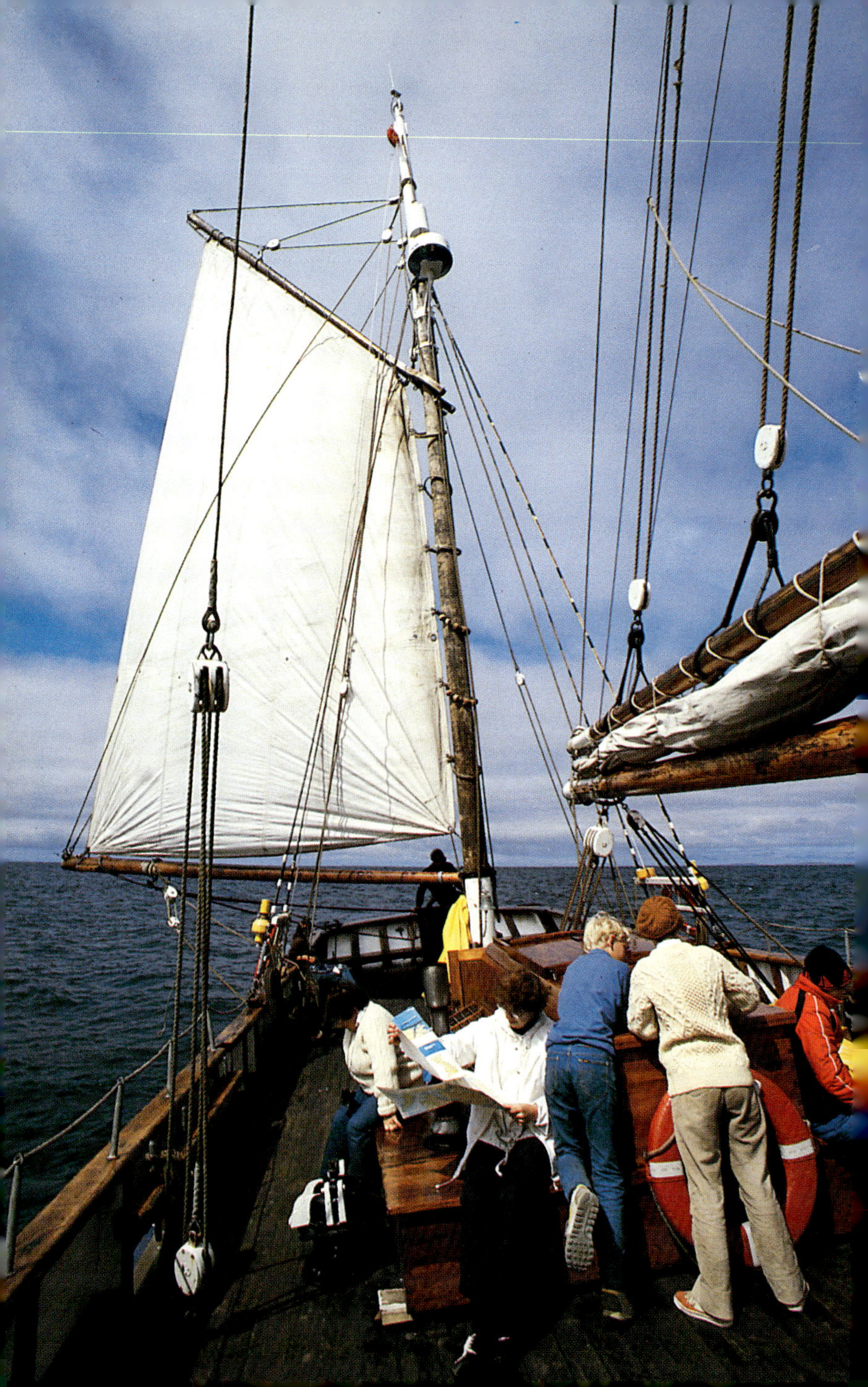

9: ACTIVITY HOLIDAYS

SOME types of holiday demand that photography comes second, however keen you may be. Paradoxically such holidays often put you in places or situations which another photographer could never hope to achieve, and even if you do not spend all day behind the camera your shots may be truly impressive.

HIKING and walking holidays are ideal for photography, with the weight of the kit kept strictly to a minimum. A compact 35mm is ideal, and so are specialist systems such as the Leica M-series rangefinder camera and lenses which take up very little space. The Olympus 35mm SLR range has been designed for minimum weight and size and is popular with anyone obliged to wear a backpack all day.

The best choice of lenses is a general purpose wide-angle like a 28mm, and a lightweight zoom from 75-150mm. A monopod (like the leg of a tripod fitted with a camera adaptor at the top) can be used as a walking-stick and some even have shooting-stick style seats available. To distribute weight, the camera and lenses can be worn in shaped pouches on a belt, or on the hip in a kind of holster. Some special back-packs have a fitted camera section with a large expandable upper part for clothes or a tent.

Any holiday on foot puts you right in touch with the scenery. A drystone wall becomes a foreground to a view, and you are so close to the subject that you can pick just which stones you prefer. A photographer in a car may travel a long way between seeing an interesting view and finding a place to park.

The walking day is a long one, and you may see very early morning light which others miss, as well as sunset.

CYCLING is almost as good as way to find landscape photographs as walking, but you are restricted to roads. Your camera kit can be held in a special kind of shaped, rigid case which straps to the body as well as over the neck and shoulder, and is designed not to cause any injury should you fall on it. Foam padding inside prevents any vibration from damaging the camera. It is not a good idea to cycle with a camera loose round your neck or held firmly to the bicycle. Any case in contact with the frame must be well padded.

MOTORCYCLE touring is probably less satisfactory than any other form of lightweight travelling with a camera. It is dangerous to use any kind of case

Duncan McEwan photographed activity on deck using a 17mm wide-angle lens during a trip on the Lorne Leader, a sailing vessel cruising in the Western Islands of Scotland.

worn on the body, even the contoured types intended for cyclists, and under no circumstances should any camera equipment be held in a pannier regardless of how much padding you give it. To shoot pictures on the move you will have to extract your camera from a backpack (the safest position) after removing your helmet. It's still a great way to travel!

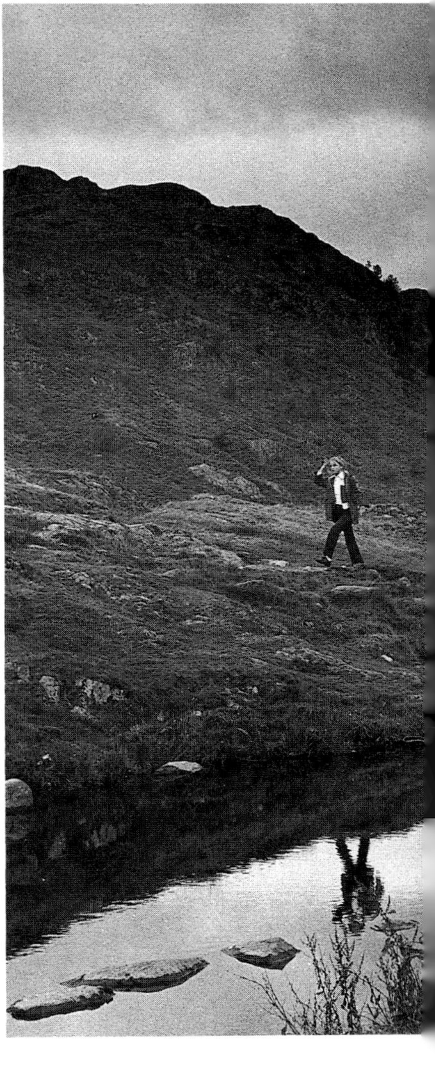

CAMPING adds more to this type of holiday. You may reach your destination by car or rail, but once a tent is pitched you have freedom to explore the countryside. Tents are not secure places to leave equipment, so you have to use a similar outfit to someone walking, light enough to be with you all the time.

Camping allows you to be further from civilization if you choose to be. A walking holiday between guest houses means that a certain distance must be covered; when camping, you can remain where you are as long as a suitable site can be found to pitch your tent. The one essential extra in your camera case is a polythene bag to place the entire photo kit in if heavy rain should penetrate the tent.

CARAVAN holidays (touring) give you a reasonably secure place to keep extra lenses, plenty of film, a tripod and similar accessories. Your stopping-places are limited, but as with camping they are

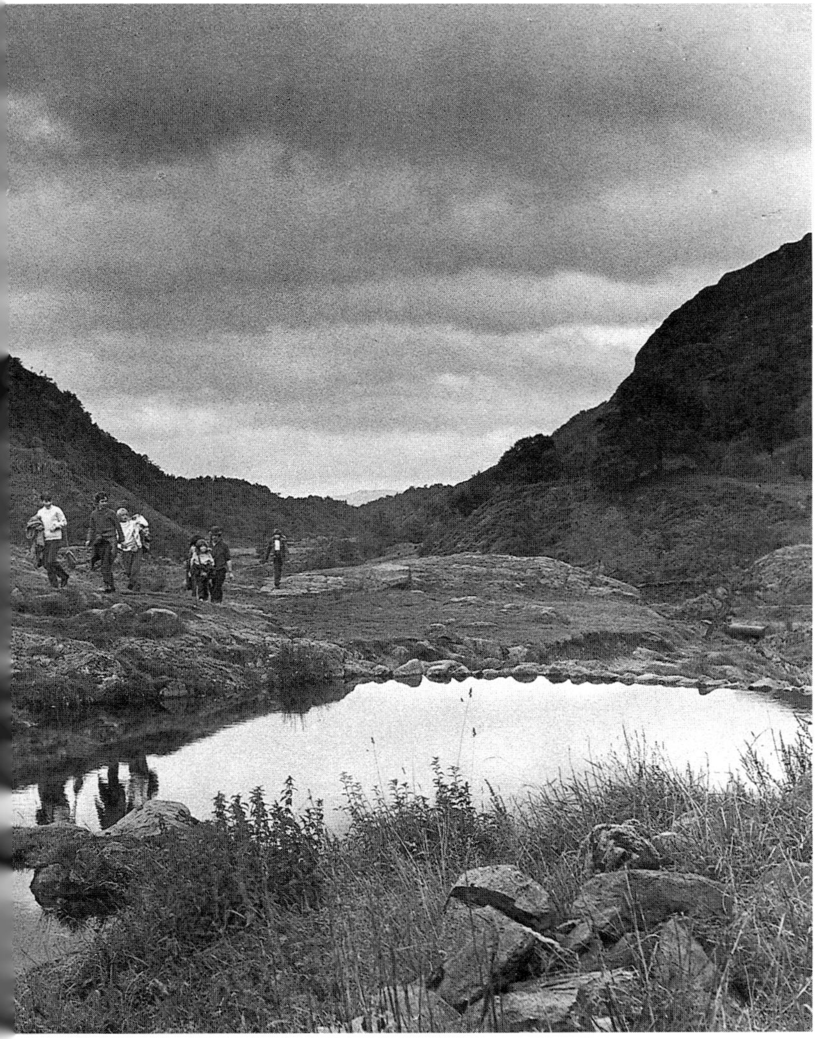

Monochrome makes a good medium when hiking or walking in Britain – it can cope with unseasonable weather and produce dramatic prints. Shirley Kilpatrick photographed Watendlath, Cumbria, on FP4 film.

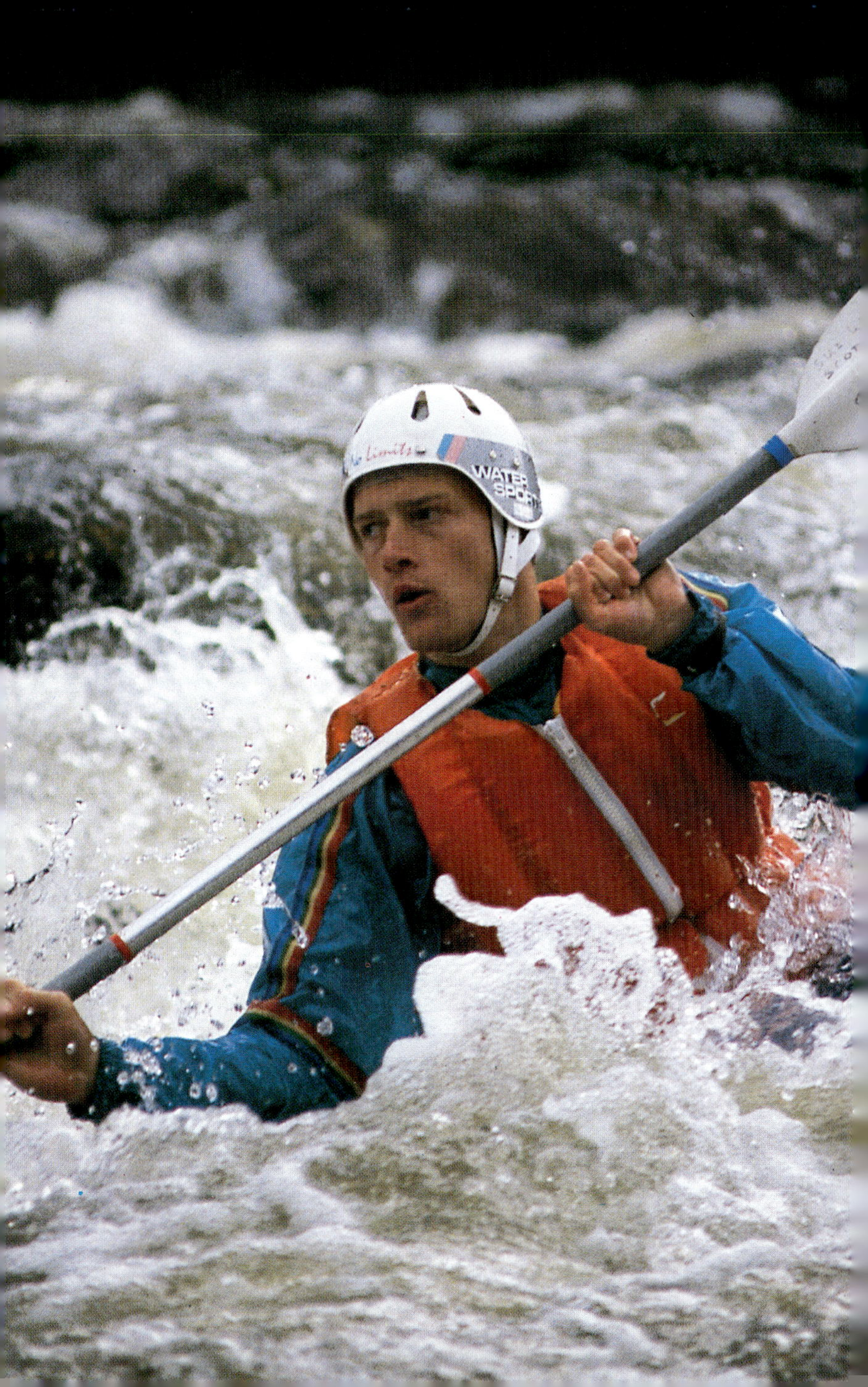
WATER

IN THE SADDLE

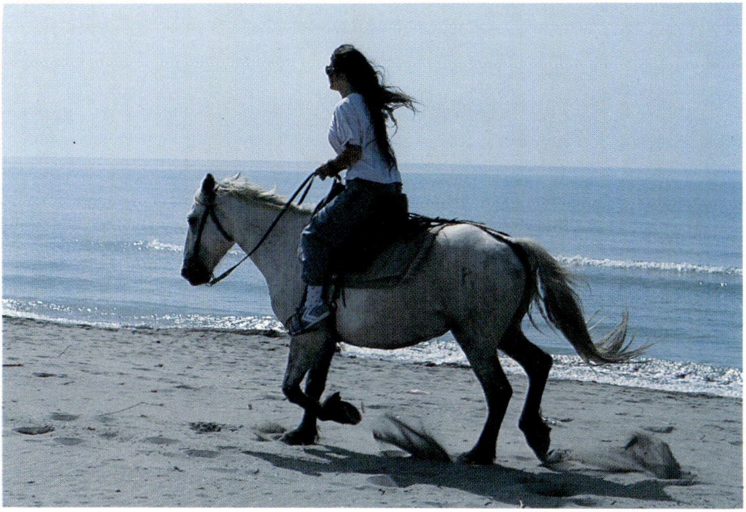

Riding in the Camargue, Shirley left her camera behind, as the horses cross sea channels and salt beaches.- David followed on foot and by car to take pictures using a 70-210mm zoom lens.

often in picturesque surroundings. The main problem with caravan touring is that you can't make sudden stops to shoot pictures when en route, and some roads are just not accessible to the caravan. You have to plan your visits to narrow mountain passes during days when your caravan will be parked.

RIDING on horseback is completely compatible with photography, using a case which can be strapped to the body rather than slung over the neck and shoulder. A belt-fitting holster case holding a camera with a wide to tele zoom is ideal. Autofocus cameras help a great deal, with single-handed operation. The horse provides a wonderful viewpoint, high enough to look right over fences and hedgerows, and can cross almost any terrain.

One of the best places to try a horseback 'safari' with a camera is the Camargue in France, where the guide will take you up to knee-height in salt water and the camera must be protected against splashes. On this particular trip a longer lens, such as 70-210mm zoom, is essential to photograph the wild horses, bulls, otters and bird life. To enjoy the ride, leave your camera behind!

RALLYING and serious motor touring do not fit in well with photography if time-limits and objectives are to be met. 'Grand touring' at leisure is a different matter. The only reasonable way to incorporate photography into cross-country rallying is to go along as a third party, unwelcome because of the weight and impossible in some classes of rally car. You can then record the total concentration of driver and navigator and the fleeting glimpses of uncharted forest through muddy windows.

CANOEING – even white water – is a popular holiday sport in Europe and the USA. Many canoeists take cameras with them in the certain knowledge that at some stage the camera will be submerged along with the canoe and their entire survival pack. As canoeing is often done in stages and the group will tackle the stage in sequence, you may be able to take good photographs of your companions from land. The only cameras suitable for photography when afloat are underwater and all-weather models, preferably with one-handed AF operation. Waterproof pouches are available from good outdoor sports suppliers and can be used to protect other cameras when in transit in the canoe.

CAVING is very similar in hardware requirements to canoeing, and it is frequently necessary to wade or even dive; many areas are wet. The opportunities for hand-held photographs are limited in the extreme. Serious cave photographers will use a special waterproof case (Pelican or Andiamo) to carry an SLR outfit. In practice larger film formats are often used, especially 6 x 6cm rollfilm, as the fine detail inside caves is a vital aspect of record photography.

Lighting inside caves can be provided by ordinary electronic flash, which must be kept strictly away from water. Each member of the team takes a small flashgun, and for a major cave photograph they position themselves all round the cavern and fire several flashes from each position while the photographer leaves the shutter open for several minutes. Because electronic flash is very low-powered for this type of work, serious cavers use flash bulbs – large, expensive and usable once only. A network of wires connects firing units for these bulbs to the camera, and only one exposure is made. The best results are spectacular and the skills required are those of the architectural photographer.

CLIMBING and mountaineering call for lightweight cameras of the same type as those suitable for walking, and favour one-handed autofocus models. The typical proximity of members of a team

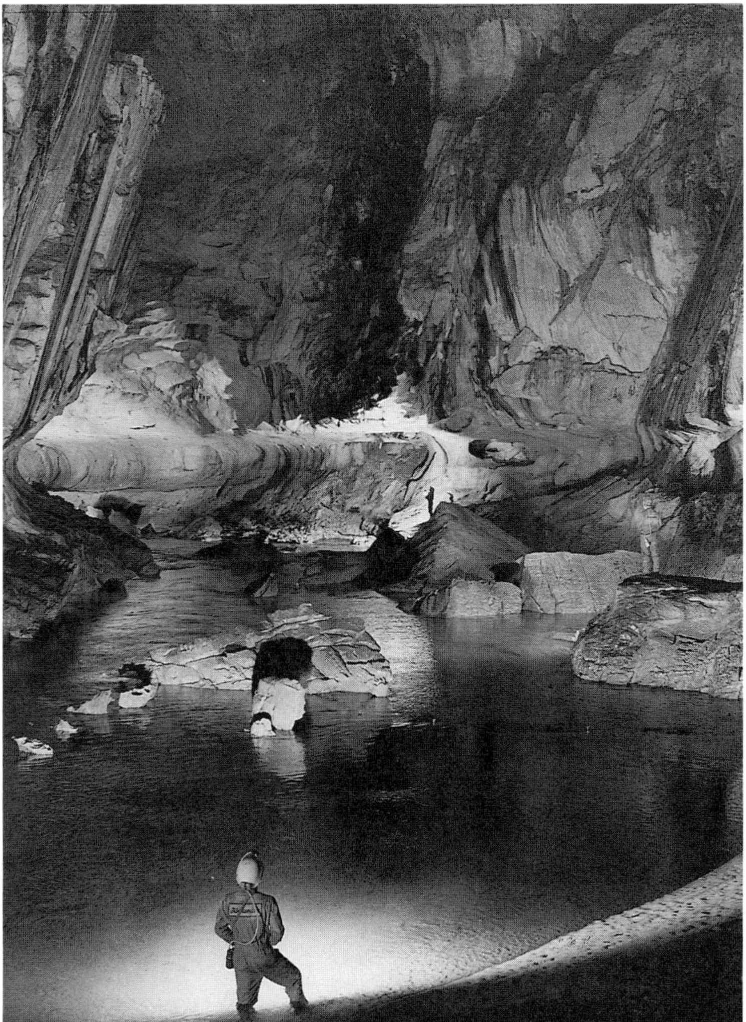

Serious cavers use large cameras – this spectacular shot of Clearwater Cave in Mount Mulu National Park, Borneo (now a tourist attraction) was taken by Jerry Wooldridge FRPS using a Bronica SQa 6 x 6cm SLR.

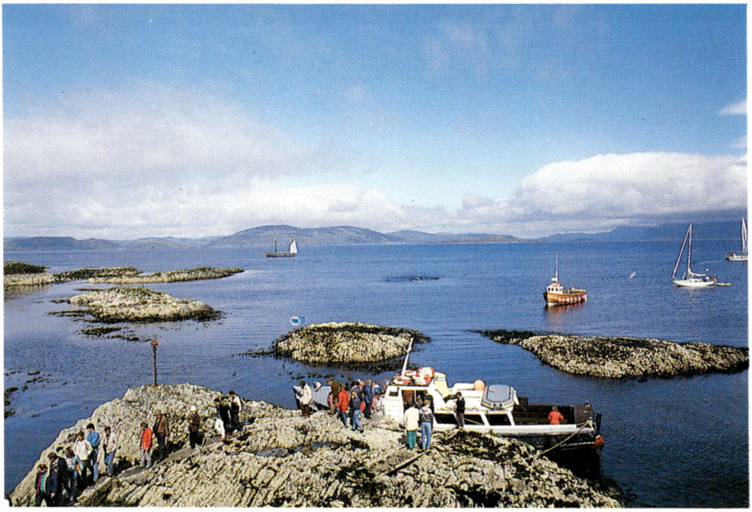

Duncan McEwan used a 24mm lens for a panoramic view from land, below, looking out towards moored sailing vessels. David Kilpatrick placed his camera on its back with a 17mm lens to record the dome of the baroque church in Pöllau, Austria.

means that the standard lens is a fairly good choice, with wide-angles around 35 to 28mm valuable for overall scenes and long focus lenses of 85-135mm good for close-ups. Some of the best mountaineering shots are taken with simple techniques and rely on circumstances which the layman finds impossible to believe for their impact. It is a very good idea to fit a rubber lenshood and a soft case to your camera when climbing.

SAILING on any reasonable scale, from individual dinghies to flotilla yachts in the Greek islands, offers excellent photographic opportunities. The best lens for photography on board larger yachts is the 24mm wide-angle. This allows on-deck and below-decks pictures with groups of people, and gives a realistic impression of the scale of the vessel. On very much smaller craft, and even wider-angle lens can be used.

Flotilla sailing gives you the chance to photograph other yachts alongside you, and here a lens of around 70-210mm zoom is ideal. Single handed operation is always valuable on board, as it allows you to steady yourself with

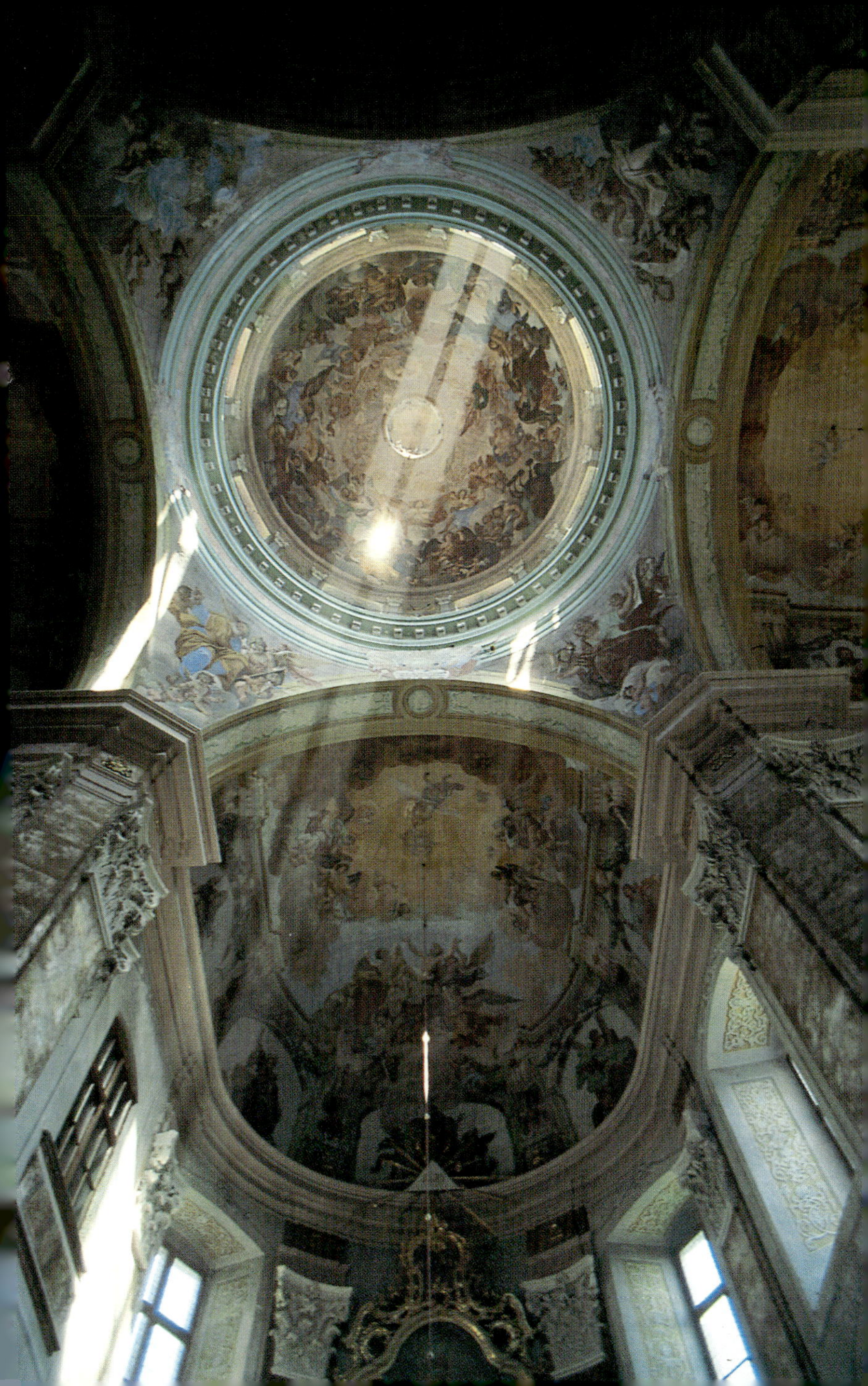

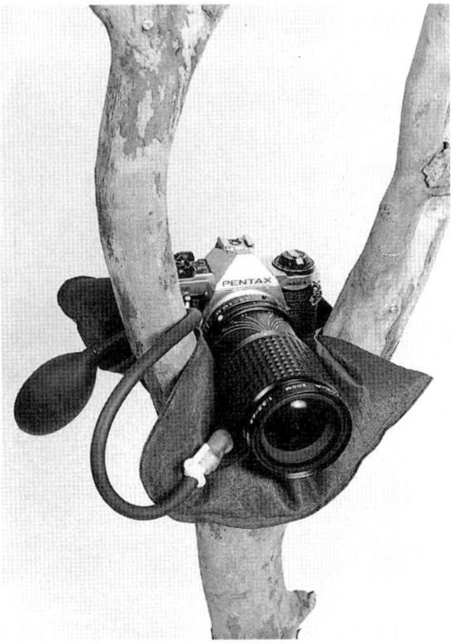

The bean-bag is a useful idea for safari and natural history photography. It allows you to stabilize a long telephoto lens on any convenient surface, such as a tree, wall or car door (photo: Jessop).

the other hand. A tripod is of little value, as all it can do is keep the deck and the camera steady in relation to each other; the horizon can continue to move freely!

Some sailing holidays, such as those offered on vessels like the Lorne Leader in the Western Isles of Scotland, involve a degree of voluntary seamanship shared between members of the group on board. All the tasks involved in the day-to-day sailing can be documented, and the many islands visited on a week's cruise of this type provide landscape, natural history, candid and every other imaginable genre of photograph.

GLIDING provides a magnificent aerial view – but your camera may have to be specially mounted, using a glass port rather than perspex to view through, and perhaps controlled by a long electrical cable release. A two-man glider offers scope for a pilot and photographer. In some ways light aircraft are better for photography. An overwing aircraft, like the Cessna 150 series, can be repeatedly banked, circled and temporarily wing-dipped to allow pictures to be taken through the opened co-pilot's window.

A hot air balloon is the ultimate aerial photography platform, and in some places you can take a short trip aloft. This is a popular way of seeing some African game reserves, but the cost of the trip is about the same as the 70-210mm zoom lens you will need for the best pictures. A wide-angle is useful for photographing the balloon itself.

PAINTING holidays need a camera more than any. In popular areas for sketching and painting, like Devon in the UK or Tuscany in Italy, you can join classes with proficient artist-teachers. It is surprising how many artists use a camera to take a series of pictures when working on preliminary sketches in the field, and refer to these later on when finishing the picture in the studio.

Painting and sketching holidays in general are excellent for photographers (given any degree of skill) and can improve your composition, use of colour, and perception of images.

CULTURAL tours also call for a camera, but few people take the right equipment. The roof and dome of a baroque church may demand an extreme wide-angle lens with the camera itself placed on its back, on the floor, looking upwards. A 17mm (the widest lens normally available in most systems) is even better than a 20mm (considered extremely wide in angle). A tripod is essential, though you may be prevented from using it in some buildings where the floor could be damaged.

In some museums and art galleries, electronic flash is banned because of potential damage to dyes and pigments caused by the ultra-violet content, and the nuisance caused to other visitors. It isn't good etiquette to use flash in churches. Always put something in the box for the building restoration fund – that way there will be something to photograph in future.

The quality of slides offered for sale in many places is much higher than it used to be, and sets can be bought for a minimal cost which show paintings or rooms which you cannot photograph yourself. These can be added to your own slide shows as long as you do not make any commercial gain from using them.

Outfits

The idea of most activity and interest holidays, other than purely photographic ones, is to join a group with a common interest and concentrate on this. It pays to keep your photographic equipment to the minimum, avoid ostentation, and put photography into second place as far as the rest of your party is concerned.

Protection

For outdoor activities, look at the cases and holdalls available from specialist camping and photo bag manufacturers. These include Tenba, Camera Care, Billingham, Fogg, Oyster, Adiamo, Pelican and a large number of others. They differ from ordinary camera cases in price, durability and the weatherproof, shockproof materials used in construction.

Special equipment

There are one or two accessories which travelling photographers find useful if an outfit has to be kept small. These include:

* Camera clamp or mini tripod
* Monopod

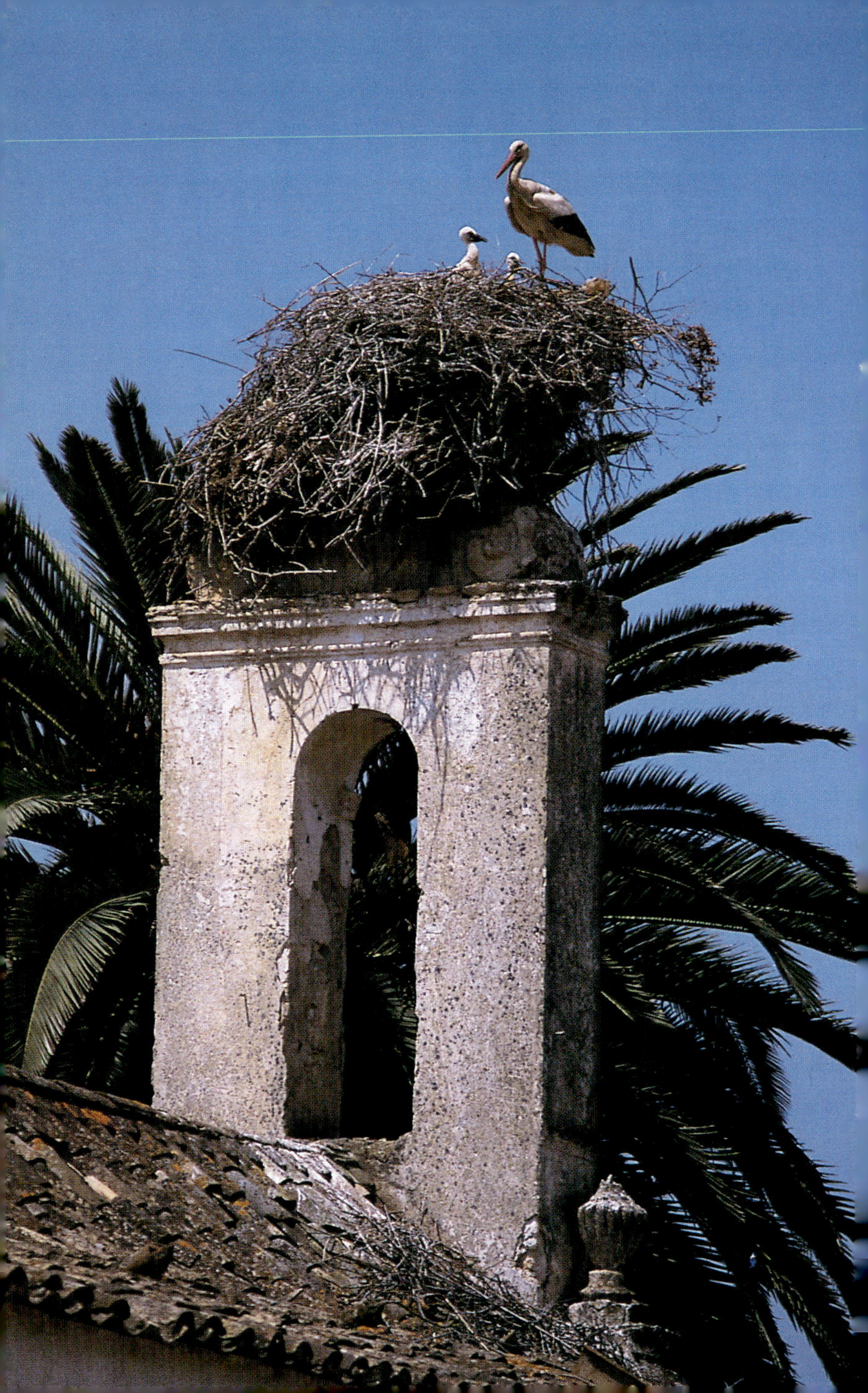

* Waterproof film canisters
* Wide neck straps
* Inflatable lens pouches
* Camera cleaning kit
* 'Bean bag'

The last item is interesting for wildlife safari holidays; it consists of a small fabric bag filled with free-flowing grains. A long telephoto lens can be cradled on the bag, rested on the side of a vehicle, a branch or a rock. The bag firms up as you compress the grains. Some have a suction pump to do this more effectively.

Fast films

Most activity holidays involve action, often without sunshine. Our normal advice on buying film is to choose ISO 100 or slower for routine holiday photography; for activity-based holidays, ISO 200 film may be better. Reserve fast films (ISO 400 to 1000) for action shots, dull days and dim interiors where no tripod or flash is permitted.

Single-handed cameras

Throughout this section, the advantage of the so-called 'one-touch' or single handed compact AF camera or AF SLR has been mentioned. The requirements for any single-handed camera are auto exposure, autofocus or fixed focus, auto film wind and possibly auto rewind and flash switch-on when the light becomes too dim.

All these features can be found in many cameras. For very unusual activities, like skydiving, which are hardly ever the basis for holidays or trips, cameras like this can be attached to a helmet and fired via a switch and cable running through your sleeve!

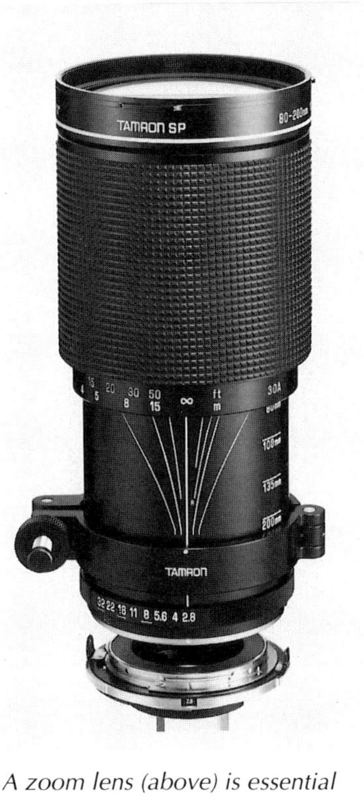

A zoom lens (above) is essential for photography in wildlife parks. The stork's nest, left, was taken in the Algarve using a 75-300mm lens at its longest focal length – only just adequate.

10: FREELANCING

FREELANCE photography has considerable attractions for keen amateurs, especially now that automatic cameras and improved films make pictures taken on most 35mm equipment 'professional' in standard. You may have looked at travel photographs in brochures and wondered where the tour companies obtain their pictures from. Perhaps you could earn some money by supplying the same kind of picture?

The short answer is that you would be very unlikely to earn anything. The travel business is divided into three sections – small independent specialist companies which do not use brochures, minor tour companies which produce leaflets and simple colour brochures, and major operators with substantial and regularly updated catalogues.

The only active market for amateur pictures is the middle one. These companies cannot often afford to commission professional photography, and tend to rely on their own staff, local photographers at the holiday destinations, picture libraries and some professionals who do a small amount of travel photography in exchange for the travel facility itself.

These companies often run photographic tours and other specialist trips, so you will have competition. You may have that in the most literal sense – some tour operators run photo contests with prizes. In short, the most likely 'market' for freelance holiday photography is the tour operator without a budget to pay for it. You may be paid a small sum, given a discount on a future booking, or perhaps just a by-line on the photograph in the brochure.

Even holidays further afield cannot guarantee any success in photo competitions. So many people on these trips are keen photographers that the photo magazines, picture libraries and travel publications receive more pictures than they can ever hope to use. Having said this, the majority of these pictures are unsuitable for commercial use anyway, though if you know what to take you can be successful in paying for part of your annual holiday.

Selling pictures

The best way to sell any photographs is to find someone who is already buying the same kind of picture and offer an alternative source. This way, the going rate is already established and the budget exists. This is how picture libraries work.

To place pictures with a library, you must take transparencies, and they must be 35mm full-frame or larger, on the right kind of film. The most popular films are Kodachrome 25, Kodachrome 64, Ektachrome 64, Ektachrome 100, Fujichrome 50 and Fujichrome 100. Slower

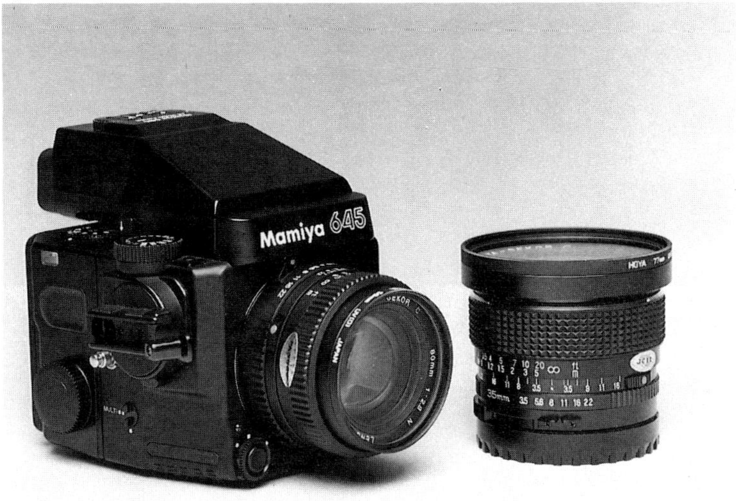

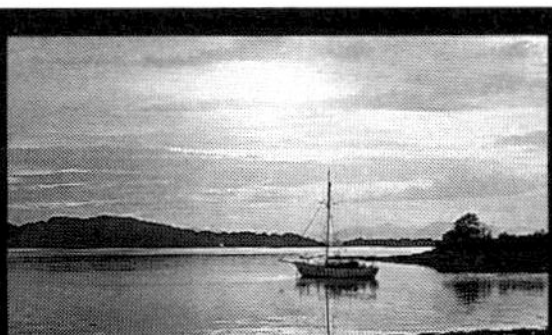

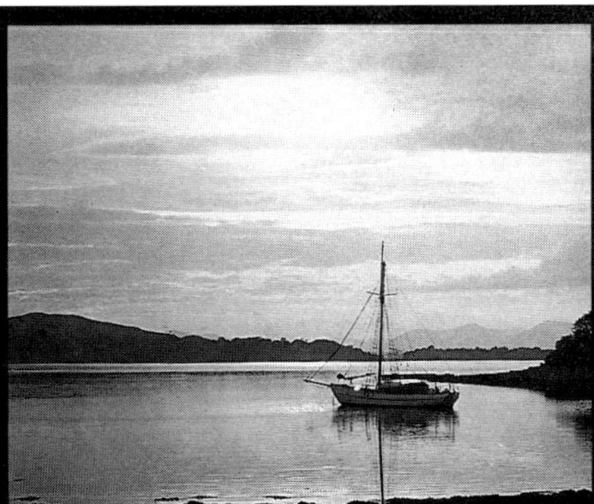

ABOVE: the normal 35mm film frame
RIGHT: rollfilm 6 x 6cm is over four times as large

The costs of cameras and film are in proportion

The freelance holiday photographer needs larger format equipment, like the 6 x 4.5cm Mamiya, top. The size of the film format, bottom, is very important to printers and designers.

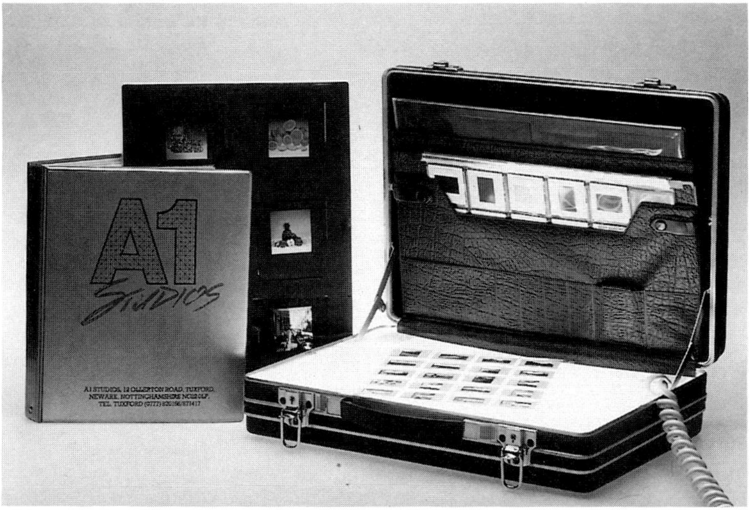

Presentation is important when you freelance. These holiday slides are presented in black mounts for rollfilm formats and a suspension filing sheet for 35mm slides, and viewed on a special light-box.

films are always preferred to faster, and if you are lucky enough to own a rollfilm camera, larger format slides will always sell in preference to the same subject photographed on 35mm.

Already you are forced to become a freelance photographer rather than someone just taking pictures on holiday. Would you enjoy this? With the right equipment, yes. Anyone taking a very expensive Hasselblad outfit on a holiday would be restricted and weighed down. A lightweight Fuji viewfinder camera taking rollfilm, specially intended for travel pictures, costs one-fifth of the price of a basic Hasselblad and can almost be slipped into a pocket. You need to be a reasonably experienced photographer before you can use a camera like this proficiently.

Given good 35mm or rollfilm slides, they still have to be presented well. A correctly exposed and composed photograph looks better in a large black card mount than in a small slide mount, and the card mount (normally 5 x 4" in size) slips into a protective sleeve with a frosted back. Your own name and address can be printed on a small label and fixed to the back; a comprehensive but concise caption goes on the front.

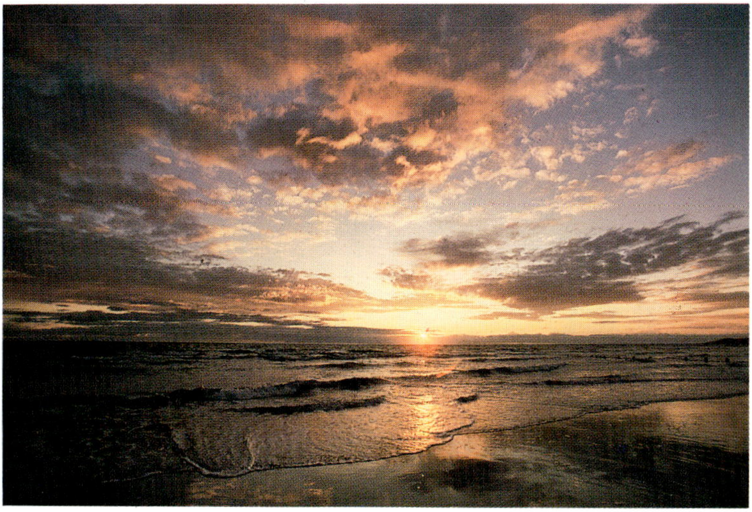

This 35mm slide of a sunset has earned well into four figures for Shirley Kilpatrick. It was submitted to Tony Stone Associates, a major photo library, in 1978; it still sells regularly ten years later.

The caption is essential for sales of travel and holiday pictures unless they show typical family scenes at unidentifiable places, or very general beach, sunset and similar themes. You should note down the country, the resort, the name of the beach if possible, the time of year, and the hotel if taken within a hotel complex.

Individual tour companies will be most interested in a set from one resort showing the hotels and beaches, trips and activities featured in their own catalogue. A set of twenty or so pictures, well packed with return postage enclosed, will be enough for their marketing department to assess.

Slide libraries will want to receive 50 to 100 different shots at a time, and will expect to keep only those which interest them – perhaps a figure as disappointing as ten per cent. This can be demoralizing at first, until you realize that the slide library genuinely expects to sell the pictures within a reasonable period several times over. Some of our own 35mm slides, taken on simple equipment and showing nothing more elaborate than a Welsh sunset or a Scottish seascape, have earned many hundreds of pounds each over a few years in a slide library.

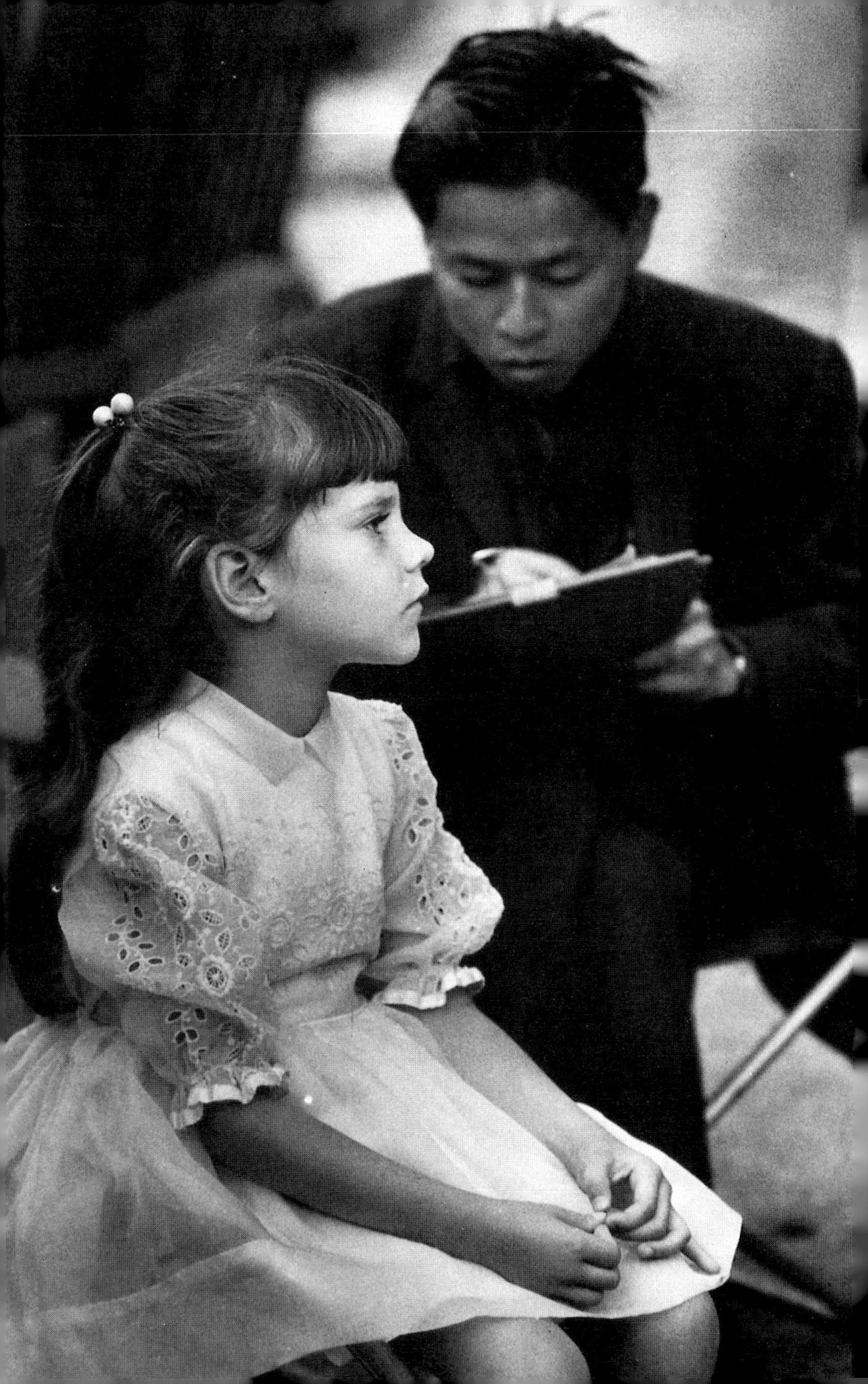

The important thing to remember is that different pictures do not sell as well as copy-cat shots. If you can imitate to perfection the pictures already appearing in brochures you will stand a better chance of having your work selected. Very often the 'rough visual' which the layout designer produces for a brochure uses pictures cut from other brochures as mock-up illustrations. The company then expects the final pictures to be similar.

Travel and general interest magazines, in contrast, want a different kind of picture. Sometimes these are black and white rather than colour, and frequently they show small details. A piece of architecture or sculpture, a chef preparing a meal, a particular water-sports location, a close-up of a flower – these can illustrate a feature on an area. Well over half the pictures used in such magazines are taken by the author of the article, or commissioned to illustrate an existing article. Pictures on their own have a very limited editorial market indeed.

Photographic magazines and contests are overwhelmed by holiday pictures, but the best pictures are still taken on holiday. They are not travel pictures – they are landscapes, close-up studies of colour, creative compositions, portraits, action shots, mood shots and indeed anything you can imagine.

The right shots

The hardest photographs for anyone to find when trying to illustrate a brochure are sometimes the easiest ones for ordinary amateur photographers to take.

Any pictures of people enjoying themselves, on the beach or at the bar, in family groups or couples, are much in demand. There is a snag. The people in the picture must look right and they must KNOW that their picture is to be used. The typical shot will have a couple aged around 30-ish (the woman may look younger) with one boy aged around eight and a girl aged around six, probably blonde, all suntanned to pleasant degree, and well-groomed. The children will be disproportionately old for their 'mother'...

The young couple running out of the waves holding hands and laughing can be younger but must still look very much Nordic – a pair of obvious Italians would not

---

If you enter photographic contests use your holidays constructively. The candid portrait study opposite was the first ever published photograph for David Kilpatrick – a first prize winner in an Amateur Photographer magazine contest back in 1970. It was taken on holiday in Paris, visiting Montmartre, with a 135mm telephoto lens.

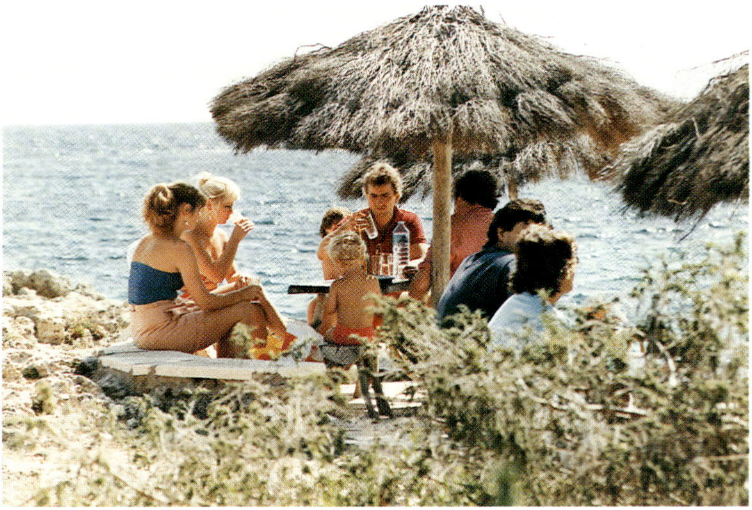

This scene of a family eating al fresco might seem harmless, but it could not be used in commercial advertising. You would have to ask permission.

fit the stereotype. Older people should be shown as couples, must have grey or white hair, look prosperous but relaxed, smile, be fairly slim, and wear casual clothes rather than a swimsuit.

Finally, you must obtain a signed model release form which allows you to sell the pictures.

This is all pretty impossible for the holiday photographer to manage. Even seasoned professionals take teams of models to shoot hundreds of slide library pictures like this, so hard are the 'right' people to find.

If you are lucky enough to see just the perfect attractive family in the ideal setting, by all means have a go – ask for co-operation and permission. The guidelines you can gather from all this are useful in general photography. You do not need model release forms when a group of people is simply fairly prominent in a general beach or pool scene, and if you make sure that the most prominent figures are generally in line with the stereotypes you will have a usable general view.

The remaining 'right' pictures are views of hotels and particular rooms, apartments or developments. There is no real point in ever taking these pictures yourself as the tour operator will have very precise requirements.

A MODEL GIRLFRIEND

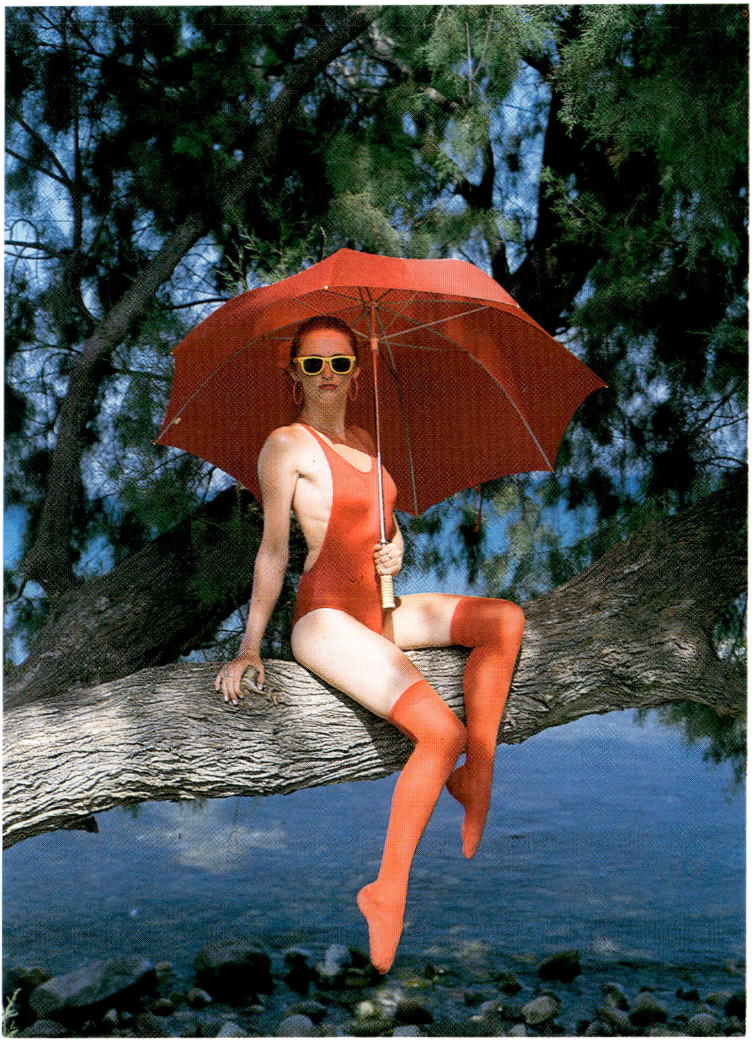

Your wife or girlfriend could be the right model. Richard Bradbury visited Kos with Caroline, above, and took brightly coloured accessories – the picture was used as a photo magazine cover.

11: USING YOUR PICTURES

BACK HOME the memories of a holiday need not fade and they certainly don't need to be kept to yourself. Other people may not be interested in your family snaps, but these days everyone travels and wants to know about interesting destinations, good hotels, lively resorts and local conditions. The old idea of the boring holiday slide-show is just not true. A good set of holiday pictures will be examined in detail by anyone thinking of going to the same place themselves.

Presenting your pictures well helps make them interesting to other people too. There are many good ways to show holiday pictures and you do not even need a slide projector!

Print albums

Processing services sometimes issue a small plastic wallet with your prints. These handy albums are easily passed round a group of people who can look at each film separately, and in many ways they are better than large albums containing all your prints. They are most certainly preferable to loose prints in a wallet, and you can label each small album with the date and place.

A better kind of album uses flip-up leaves arranged in a vertical run on a tall page. Each picture is lifted up to view the next, and a hundred or so may be accommodated in each stiff-covered album. You can use a special pen (such as the Staedtler Foto Pen) to write on the back of the colour prints without smudging. If you write the caption to each photograph UPSIDE DOWN on its back, it will be right way up when the album leaf is lifted to view the next picture.

Albums with larger leaves can take any size print, unlike the types mentioned so far which will fit either 9 x 13cm or 6 x 4". Some use a range of transparent leaves to fit various sizes like 7 x 5" and 10 x 8", others have a thin plastic cover sheet which adheres to the page and holds any combination of photographs in place. The advantage of these albums is that you can type or write small captions, keep interesting restaurant bills or menus, and make a kind of collage of all the incidental things to do with the holiday.

Slide shows

A slide show should be arranged in a logical, if not chronological, order. You should be able to give a few words of commentary during the projection which explain why each picture follows the last, and what is being shown

There is no need to have darkened rooms with modern projectors. Small free-standing screens, similar to a television in size, allow daylight projection with any ordinary projector. A family group can view these with

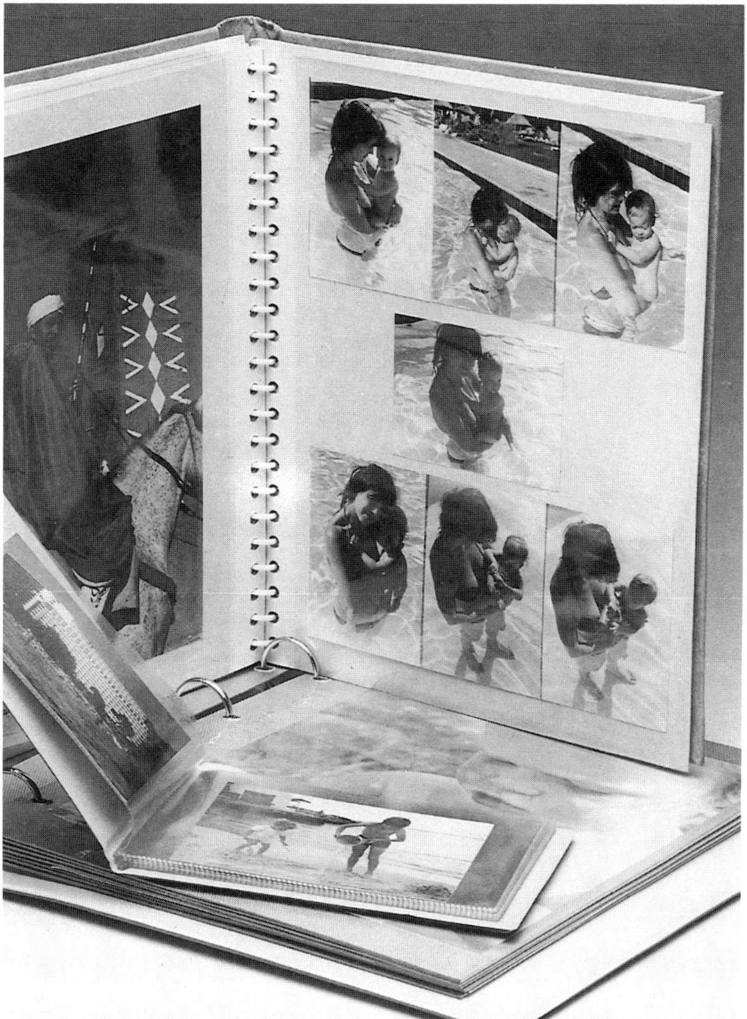

Albums for small prints range from wallets which hold only one film to flip-page books carrying hundreds. Hardback albums can fit prints up to 10 x 8" in any combination of sizes on each page.

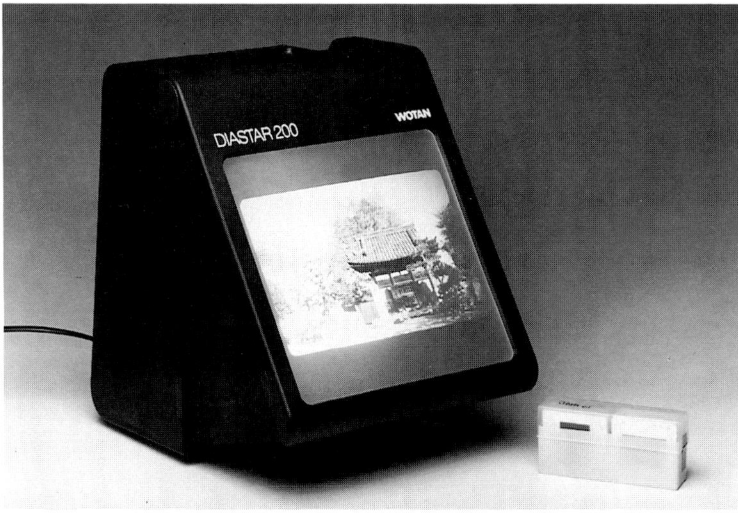

A small table-top projector with a built-in screen allows a group of people to view your slides without blacking out a whole room. Most projectors like this can also throw an enlarged image onto a screen.

greater comfort than a four-foot wide screen in a darkened room. Slide magazines hold all the slides in order, the right way up, and store them in a dust-free box. The old problems of slides inserted upside down and covered in dust or hairs need never happen.

For personal viewing, the illuminated magnifier is outdated; much better mini-projectors exist which let you put an entire boxful of loose slides into a channel and view them one by one on a small, brilliant screen. The whole area of the picture is visible without any distortion to about the same size as a double-page spread from this book.

Proper slide shows can be improved greatly by titles and captions. When you take your pictures, photograph any signs, nameplates, menus, and other details which help identify shots and make good explanatory slides. If you own a home computer try creating captions on the screen, and photograph them on to slide film using a shutter speed of around 1/15th and a tripod to ensure proper recording.

Adding sound to slide shows is easy with a stereo tape deck and a slide synchronizer which plugs in between the projector's remote control socket and the tape deck's

THE SECRET OF BRIGHT COLOURS

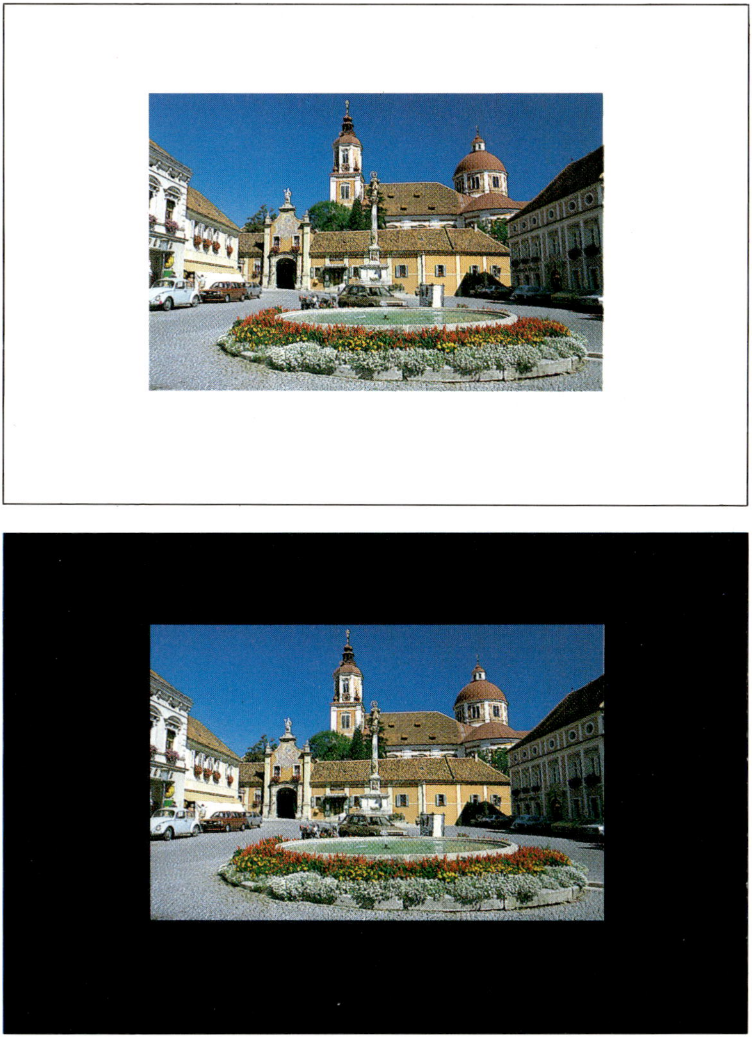

Here is why slides always look better than prints – these two colour pictures are identical. We have reproduced one against white and one against black. The colours look much brighter in the bottom shot.

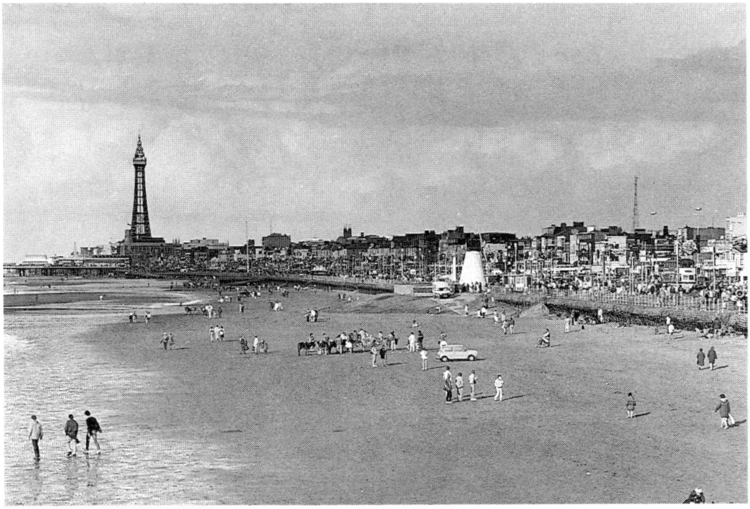

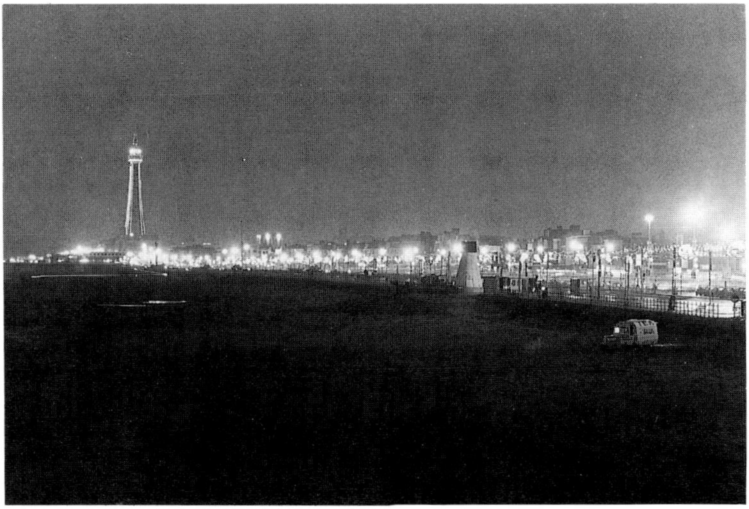

Richard Bradbury photographed Blackpool seafront by day and night from exactly the same position for the Prudential regional calendar. A slide-dissolve between these scenes would be highly effective.

output. You can buy special tape machines with a third track to allow full stereo sound; with ordinary decks, you can only use one (mono) track as the other is used by the synchronizing pulses. Local music can be recorded on holiday with a pocket tape recorder or purchased in album or cassette form. You are not allowed to use copyright music for public showing, but this does not present serious problems for non-profit-making personal enjoyment.

Slide dissolve is a more sophisticated method of projection which uses two projectors to flow smoothly from one shot to the next without a sharp transition. Many effects can be added to this including alternation between two pictures, very slow dissolves, sudden snap changes and superimposition (of captions). It is an expensive addition to your hobby but very enjoyable, and it provides you with an objective on holidays. The sequences and pairs of slides required for a good dissolve show are not the same as ordinary shots. A sunset, for example, would be photographed over a period of an hour and projected in sequence as four or five shots; a town photographed in the afternoon can dissolve to the same view at night with all the lights on. To do this perfect alignment is essential and special 'register pin' slide mounts are needed.

Pictures on video

Whether you take slides or prints or a combination of both, it is possible to have a sequence transferred to videotape for playback on your own VCR. You may want to do this yourself. The transfer services normally offer to produce a number of captions and add these to the set of pictures, and use copyright-free library music which plays unobtrusively in the background. The better services will match the mood of the music to the place you visited.

To order a video transfer, arrange your slides and prints in order and number according to the system used by the transfer service. They will provide you with an order form, which normally has space for around 120 different pictures over a 20-minute 'show'. As each service varies you will need to follow the instructions supplied.

The advantage of a video tape in place of a slide show or albums is that you can have copies made and send these to friends you met on holiday, or members of your family. Some video recorders allow you to add you own commentary to the commercially-produced tape at home after you get it back.

You may also be able to incorporate parts of video film you have taken yourself on holiday along with stills (or do vice-versa).

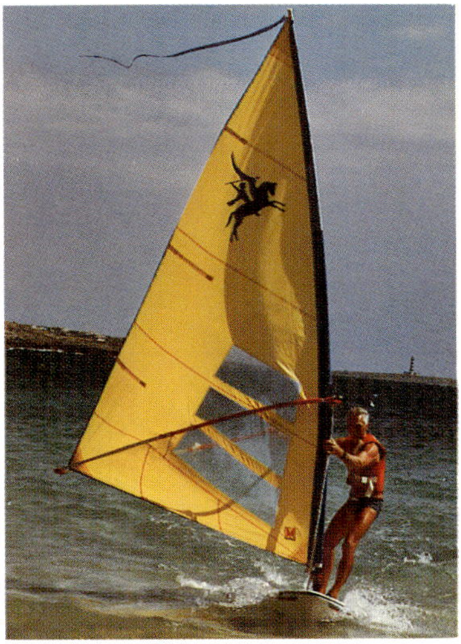

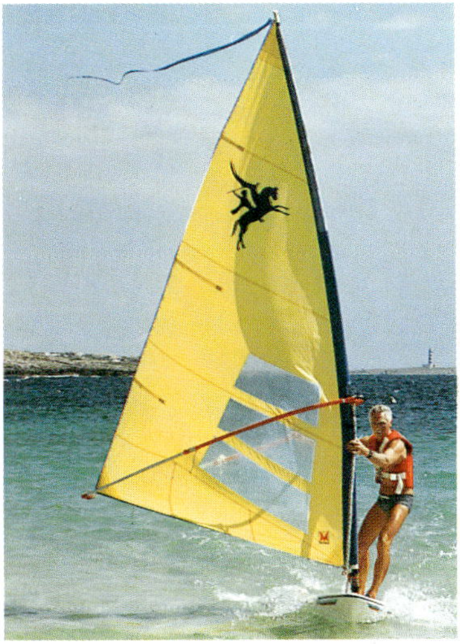

Above left is a typical machine print showing a crooked horizon, poor colour and print exposure. A better quality reprint, selectively enlarged, can correct the faults and make a good picture (above right).

Enlargements

Nothing attracts more attention than a good picture well framed and displayed. Why use other people's paintings or photographs in your home if you can use your own?

The normal maximum size for enlarging a 35mm picture is 20 x 30", which is very big indeed. Most colour negative films up to ISO 200 produce an acceptable 20 x 30" print. A better all-round size for framing is 12 x 16", which involves cropping the picture slightly. If you have a number of pictures to show, the 12 x 8" size is inexpensive and uses the whole 35mm picture, but not all colour printing laboratories offer this.

A well-composed shot can be enlarged as a MACHINE print. this means that the cropping and degree of enlargement are both fixed, and no special attention is paid to adjusting the alignment or exact framing of the picture. These prints are low in cost and the quality depends entirely on your own skill.

Selective enlarging calls for a HAND print. For two to three times the cost of machine prints, a hand print can be enlarged from any reasonable section of the original slide or negative, straightened up if the shot is

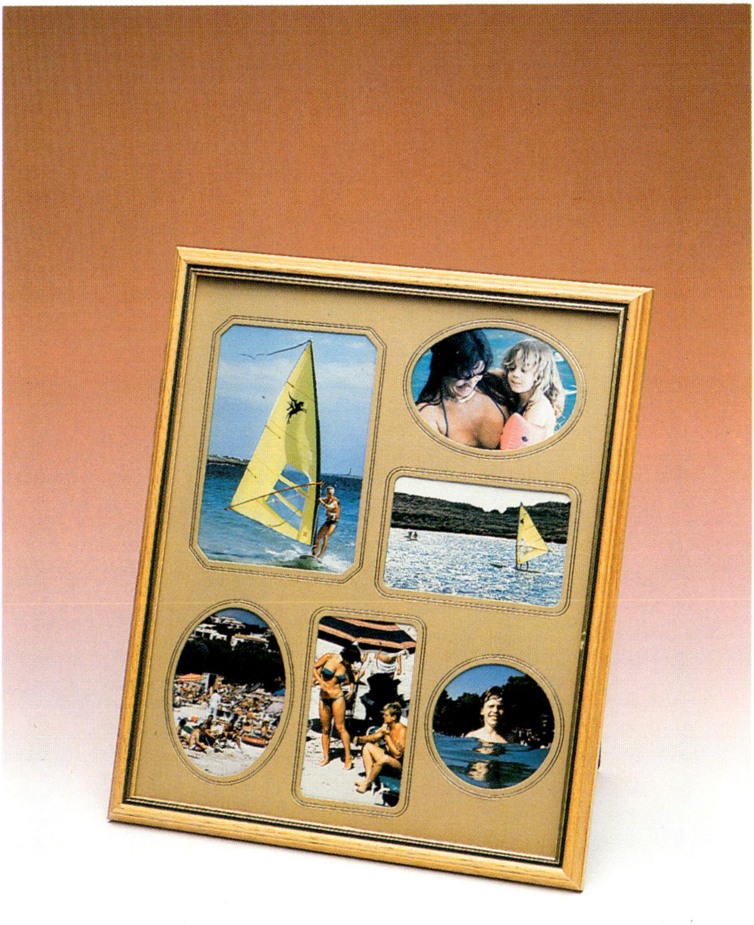

Frames don't have to be for one print only. This multi-window frame can display a set of pictures of your holiday, and the prints need only be ordinary enprints, not enlargements.

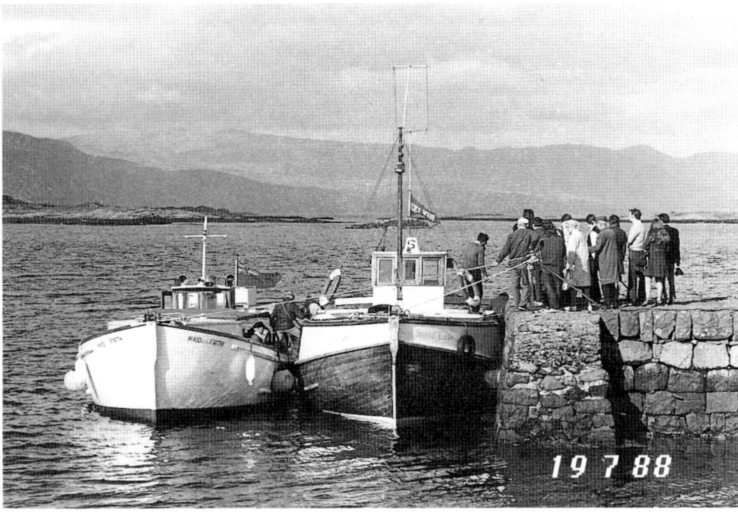

A print taken on a 35mm camera with a data back shows the day, month and year when the picture was taken – but the marking can not be removed from the negative.

crooked, and selectively adjusted in colour. A sunset can be made richer or a face in shadow lighter, without losing detail in the rest of the picture. The practical limit is that you should not enlarge anything smaller than half your negative area if you expect good results.

Dates and data

Many cameras now offer an option or facility to imprint dates or data on the frame itself, so that every print or slide has the date when it was taken permanently marked. This is a popular feature in Japan, where the majority of compact AF 35mm cameras have data backs fitted, but less so elsewhere. Perhaps the main reason is that the date cannot be removed from the picture and is often positioned well into the frame, so that it always appears on a print regardless of the size and shape.

Data backs give you a choice of printing the date, the time of day or in some cases exposure data or serial numbers. One or two expensive models print off the actual picture area, between the film frames, and can even be programmed through a small keyboard with a whole sentence. You can use data backs like this

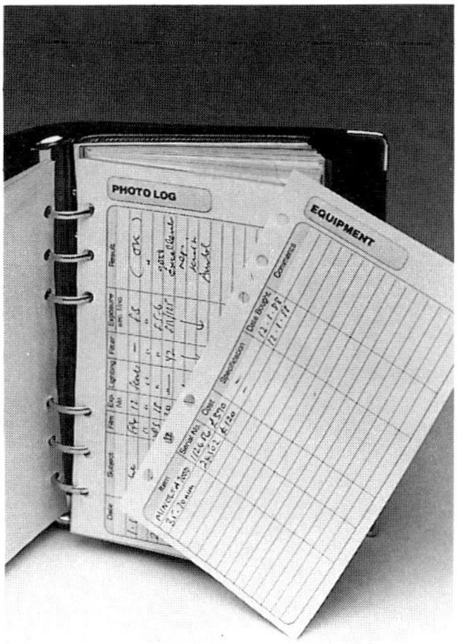

A photo log book can keep a record of all the data you need without imprinting each frame

to caption the photograph at the time you take it.

On the whole, data backs cause more problems than they are worth; the day you leave the data back switched on and take an entire film only to find each shot ruined by a large red date-stamp, you will be tempted to leave it switched off for good. It depends on what you want to do with your pictures.

You may find a date on every print the most useful feature imaginable, especially in years to come when you want to identify how old your children were and where the picture was taken. A log book can do the same job...

Editing your photographs

When other people view your pictures – in whatever form – they don't have the same interest in the ones which failed. Ruthless editing is not called for but removal of duplicate near misses and total failures IS. You do not lose anything by discarding bad prints.

Sometimes your pictures will not reach your expectations. The entire set of shots may seem to be wrong in colour, too dark, or too low in contrast. When this is the case with prints, the first thing to do is to take the whole film back to the processor and ask for it to be reprinted. If there is a genuine problem with under-exposure, an infrequent cause of these results, the second set of prints will be no better. Most of the time the fault has lain with the processor and the replacement set will be a big improvement.

Slides which are consistently wrong in exposure indicate a serious problem with the camera's metering. The only exceptions are films of snow scenes, open seascapes or beaches which have been taken with no correction applied to the exposure. One simple cause for exposure failure is incorrect setting of the ISO speed dial on the camera when the film was loaded; on one occasion we met a Mexican tourist in Spain who had visited nine countries in fourteen days and shot every single frame of Kodachrome 64 with his camera set to ISO 400.

If the editing process means removing over half your slides or prints you might consider whether the camera system you are using is the right one for you. Poor focusing can be improved with autofocus cameras; inconsistent exposures are dealt with very effectively by certain camera models which feature multi-point or contrast-balancing exposure systems.

Try totting up a simple 'success rate' score for different cameras if you own more than one, different lenses, and different types of film. You may find that sticking to a particular combination turns out a higher percentage of satisfactory results in future.

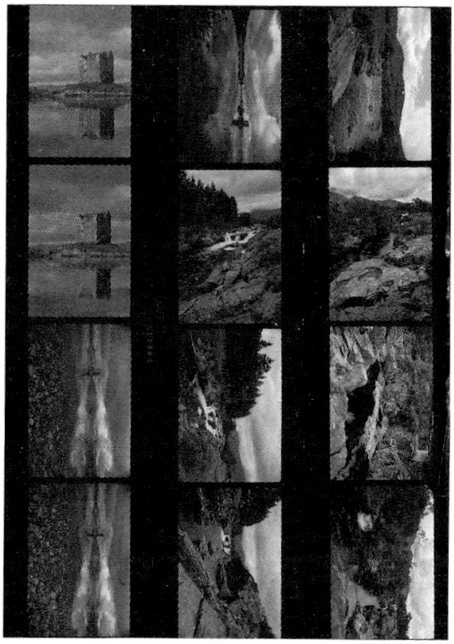

Postcards and stationery

One of the better small ideas to reach the shops recently has been photo stationery – cards with a slot or an adhesive patch allowing you to put your own prints on them. You can send postcards, greetings cards and even Christmas cards this way.

Proper postcards can be printed, too, at relatively low cost. A run of 1000 lithographically printed cards costs no more than 100 photographic reprints. If you holiday in the same place regularly, you may show a particularly good photograph to a hotel proprietor or a local shop, and perhaps the possibility of making it into a postcard could arise. The photographic magazines often carry advertisements for this service and it is not as expensive as you might assume.

Beware import regulations, however. When the English photo-journalist Peter Johns left his position with The Guardian newspaper he set up a photographic study centre in the Portugese Algarve. Over a couple of years he produced some original colour views of the area. Because the authorities insist that any postcards sold in Portugal are also printed there, he was never able to import the thousands of cards he had printed in Great Britain and put them on sale in Portugal.

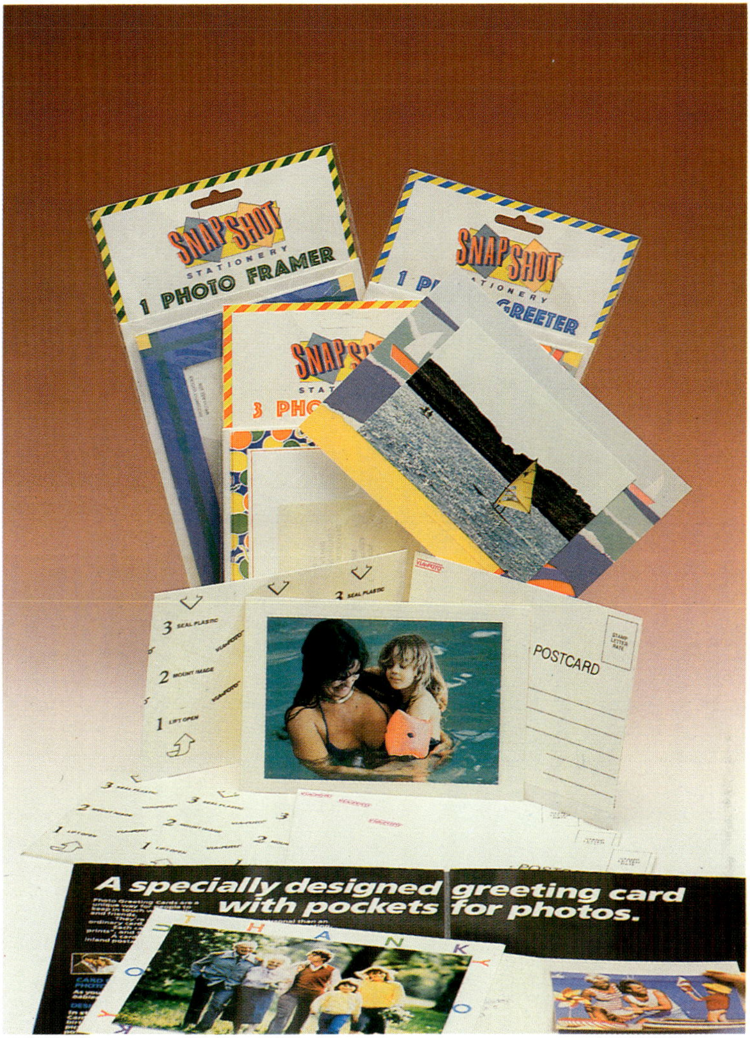

Consistent errors (opposite page) can mean equipment faults. If you forgot to send a postcard at the time, why not use photo stationery (above) and send a print afterwards in a suitable card mount?

12: VIDEO

MOVING pictures are more popular by the year as video camcorders get smaller – the Video-8 format has made holiday video movies totally practical. Don't think that taking a video camera on holiday means struggling with a large case, power packs and mains adaptors. A modern Betacam, VHS, compact VHS or Video-8 camera is significantly lighter and smaller than a 35mm SLR with a couple of lenses. Unlike a still camera, it is a complete unit and has very few accessories.

The best formats for holiday videos are the compact cassettes of videotape rather than the larger standard VHS and Betamax, though these do give higher quality. You will probably be able to play back from a true camcorder (camera-recorder with full playback or monitor facilities) using local televisions. The video signal standard in the USA is different from that in Britain and many other countries, so if your European camcorder refuses to team up with a US hotel television set, don't be surprised.

Video cameras need a little more care in handling than 35mm cameras. They are prone to damage by condensation, and should never be used when there any risk of water penetration or moisture forming inside the camera due to atmospheric conditions. The image tubes can be damaged by very bright light, and most shoulder-straps are designed so that the camcorder naturally hangs lens-down. Use the lenscap supplied and take any instructions about heat, bright light and condensation seriously.

Video camera bags

The best transit case for a camcorder is a simple shoulder-bag with fully padded walls. There is no need for this to be a rigid alloy case; fabric or leather are perfect as long as the bag has sufficient padding, and pockets to hold tapes and ni-cad batteries. Take two or three spare power packs or ni-cads with you, leaving the charger behind except on long trips. Buy a mains adaptor before leaving (most airport duty free shops have an excellent universal travel adaptor) and always check the mains voltage and polarity before connecting any equipment.

The X-ray units at airport security points should not affect your equipment or tapes in any way. Some manufacturers advise that 'magnetic media' are best taken through by hand; this is really a precaution to avoid damage to computer disks, and ordinary holiday videotapes or camera tubes and circuits should not be damaged.

Accessories

To avoid being overloaded with fragile items, leave your detachable boom microphones behind! Your most useful accessories may be a polarizing filter (rarely used in video work), a plain UV filter to protect the lens from dust, and a small sun-gun. This is the video equivalent of a pocket flashgun and will give you no more than an hour of shooting from a fully charged battery pack. A typical video sun-gun, such as a Luxfoto, Wotan or Kaiser model, is not expensive when compared with the price of your camcorder. The secret to successful use of this after-dark filming aid is to restrict yourself to short 'takes' of around ten to fifteen seconds. Never try to use a video light for shots lasting a minute or more, especially if the light is battery-operated.

The serious video user with larger equipment may want to take a good microphone, as the built-in directional mikes on most camcorders are fairly crude. To run Betamax and VHS cameras with separate recorders on location powerful battery sources are needed. A ni-cad pack may last 40 minutes or so, and the mains charger becomes a necessity.

An alternative to the ordinary battery packs can be worn round your waist. PAG power packs, and similar batteries, are used by news video cameramen. A set of batteries fits like a heavy belt, and can run a camera, recorder or video light. Professional batteries like this are not prohibitively expensive and do in fact fit many ordinary cameras via an adaptor cable. The ultimate refinement, for the travelling video enthusiast, is the PAG recharging unit which works from solar cells – while you are getting a suntan, your video camera batteries are recharging from the same source of energy!

Storyboards

A holiday video is much better if you can plan it. As most camcorders offer very limited back-wind and edit facilities, you cannot expect to adhere to a rigidly-written storyboard and make a ciné-style film of your trip. You can however keep a chronological record or a subject record at will by using a set of videotapes.

The travelogue approach – a story told from departure to return more or less as things happen – keeps you glued to the video camera all the time. This can get in the way of a family holiday more than the most dedicated still photographer's enthusiasm! If you expect to film your arrival at the airport, lugging luggage around, going through customs, boarding the plane... well, you need patient companions. Moreover, a lapse of continuity at any time during the rest of the trip will waste your early efforts.

The theme-tape approach is more fun. Using Video-8 or any tape format which is small enough, label half a dozen tapes with different subjects or ideas.

Have one tape for 'The Flavour of Spain' – put this tape in for meals, evening entertainment, bullfights, parades, and anything which fits the title. If you plan ahead, you can shoot or create a title at the start of the tape and even put the holiday dates on. When you get back you can finish the tape with a closing title.

This approach lets you set very particular projects if you know your destination. If you visit Crete you will probably go to see King Minos's palace of Knossos; a trip round this is worth a good 90 minutes of filming, particularly if you go along with a guide who will provide a built-in commentary. Keep a blank tape specially for such a tour, starting it only when you reach the location and can shoot the road signs pointing the way and opening distant views of the place.

If you like playing with simple film-scripts, try shooting a video to accompany a piece of music which you like. Make a note of the lengths of each passage in the music and the mood or theme you have in mind; photograph clouds, waves coming in, circling gulls, sunsets, waving grasses, and any other images which seem to suit it. Match your shot lengths to the music and put the two together when you get home. You may be able to evoke a powerful impression of 'place' in this way by picking the right music to go with the type of images you can find.

Video shots

There are many specific techniques you can use to enliven a holiday video. A description of video techniques and shots would take several chapters. In practice, you can use one or two standard ideas to ensure that your video looks 'right'.

Continuity is the art of ensuring that things do not change suddenly between shots. If someone leaves the picture at the right, the next shot should show them entering from the left unless you want to convey the impression that they are coming back. If a table is set with food and appears in the next shot with all the food eaten, you will raise a laugh rather than convey the impression that the meal is over. You must show people eating in between the two shots.

Static shots are generally preferable to moving-camera shots. If you can use a support or tripod, do so. The power zoom on your camera is set by the manufacturer to a zooming rate which looks natural, so use it. Manual zooms at faster speeds look disastrous unless they are 'snap' zooms, so quick that you hardly see them. Panning (moving the camera across a scene) should only be done at slow speeds, with the lens set to a wide-angle view.

If you want to pan from one

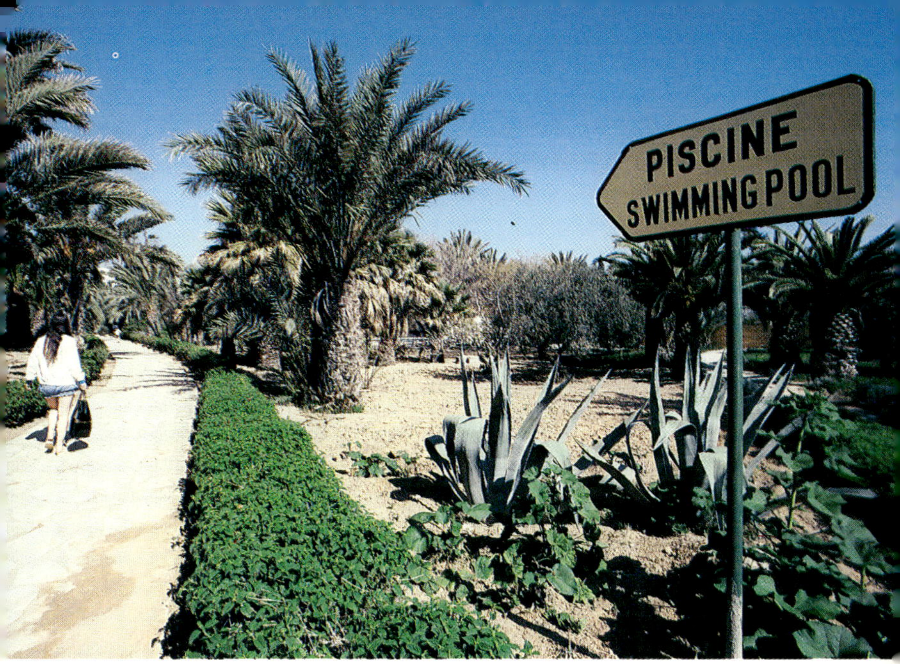

Use a shot of a sign to open a sequence – 'on the spot' titles

small close-up detail to another in a single shot, start filming with the close-up detail already framed. Carefully zoom back out to show the overall scene, and simultaneously pan the camera gently round so that the new subject is centred; then zoom in, adjusting the camera to ensure that when you have reached the correct degree of magnification the framing is correct.

Avoid shooting from moving cars, trains or coaches. If you are on a fairground ride or in a cable-car, try shooting just for effect; the movement will be very different, and may give an impression of wild activity or peaceful swaying respectively. Always look for action in the scene, rather than action from the camera – a water-skier rushing past looks good even in the static shot.

Use dissolves and fades sparingly. If every shot is linked by a dissolve, the video becomes boring. A ratio of one dissolve to every two snap cuts between scenes is OK; if you have a variable dissolve available, use a fast setting most of the time. Long slow dissolves or wipes between scenes are confusing; fade-out/in is worse, as the screen is blank for too long. Most simple cameras without any post-editing will allow you to create a simple preset dissolve or fade effect. Clean snap cuts between scenes are more important in many ways, and cameras without this create disjointed and amateurish videos.

13: MAKING YOUR OWN PRINTS

DARKROOM work has less appeal in an age of automatic cameras and colour films than it did when black and white was the most popular photographic medium. It does nevertheless offer great advantages and enjoyment to anyone prepared to make the necessary preparations.

You do not need to own a darkroom to do your own processing. There are hobby darkroom centres in many cities which can be rented by the hour, with or without instruction. You use an individual enlarger and share automatic processing machines, removing the need to mix or handle any chemicals.

The main advantage given by printing your own negatives is that you can judge how to crop, adjust or compose the shot and whether or not the colour should be changed. The quality obtained is often much higher than the standard machine 'enprint' from a d & p service. It is possible, of course, to adjust the colour incorrectly, print the negative out of focus and end up with a worse result instead. If you find yourself unable to judge whether or not things are right, it may be better to use commercial laboratories.

D & P: judging standards

Developing and printing services remain the best way to have your film processed to start with. No matter how good you are in the darkroom, the requirements for processing slides or negatives (the film) are so stringent that a one-shot manual process with a developing tank can never compete with large automatic machines. Nor can you make 24 or 36 prints of acceptable quality, at a small size, and match the price you pay for this service by mail or over a shop counter.

Once you have the negatives and prints (or slides) you can see which pictures are best, and you have a good starting-point to judge and compare the colour and density. Take the print with you into the darkroom, and use it to help you make an enlargement. By far the best sizes to try first are 7 x 5" and 10 x 8", the former being made two-up on the 10 x 8" sheet of paper.

You should choose the best d & p service you can find, to ensure that your slides are developed to the maximum colour saturation and purity, and your negatives are clean and free from scum or scratch-marks. How the service treats your film is a good indication of its quality.

Very basic, poor-quality services often:

* Mount all slides with no *unmounted* option

* Cut negatives into strips of four and attach a paper carrier

* Leave the strips loose and unprotected in a section of the print wallet

* Ask you to cut the negatives into single frames for reprints

Semi-professional services normally:

* Offer unmounted slide processing, returning the film in a sleeved roll or cut and inserted into clear filing sheets

* Cut negatives into strips of six and insert into a filing sheet or sleeves

* Enclose an order form for reprints asking you to quote which frame is to be enlarged or printed using the film's frame number

There is a substantial difference in cost between the worst and best. Look for those laboratories which claim to offer a special grade of service for the photographic enthusiast at a slightly higher price, and issue a price list which includes larger machine prints and hand prints. You may spend twice as much on having your holiday films processed but the results will be far better.

If you intend to print from your slides rather than project them, ask for unmounted processing. This avoids any risk of incorrect cutting-up, scratching or other damage to the film during the mounting process. If you want to make a contact-sheet from your colour negatives rather than use enprints as a basis to assess them, ask for developing only – but remember that the difference in price is hardly worth it. You might as well save time and effort and have the prints to keep – they are better than a contact sheet.

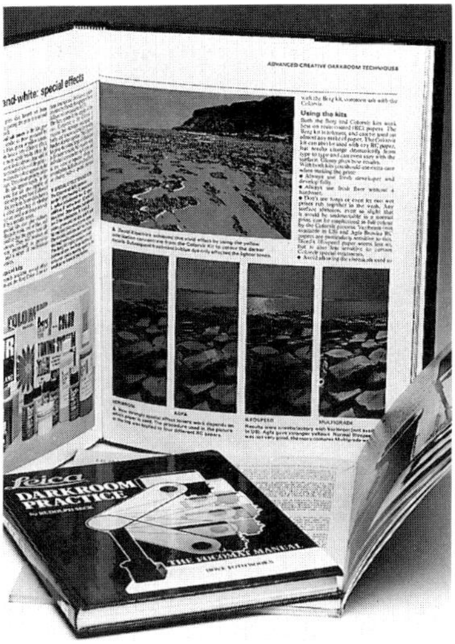

Books on darkroom methods help you plan your first efforts and design your working area

Making your own prints

Before making your own prints, buy some books on darkroom work and attend an evening class or photographic society which instructs beginners in darkroom methods. You are likely to receive considerable help and support from other people and you may be able to see how they have set up their own darkrooms and what kind of results they achieve.

Printing from slides is simple using materials like Cibachrome. You have little to worry about in terms of colour balance adjustments, and the processes are tolerant. Cibachrome is an expensive material and each 10 x 8" print made from a slide in this way will cost as much as a similar 10 x 8" commercially produced from a negative.

Printing from negatives is increasingly simple, as films are now very consistent and the paper, chemicals and enlargers have all improved beyond recognition since the early 1970s when home colour enlarging became popular.

The cost of a 10 x 8" colour print from a negative is around the same as the cost of a 6 x 4" colour reprint made commercially, and the average time taken for each finished print is around ten to fifteen minutes. Your first one will take you an hour or two, and may involve throwing away half a dozen sheets of paper in the process of mastering exposure times and colour filtration settings. After this you should rapidly become more economical!

A home darkroom

The basic requirement for a home colour darkroom is a room around eight by six feet – a large boxroom or small bedroom – with or without running water. You will need a tap to wash your prints and obtain the water for mixing chemicals, but the actual process does not call for plumbing. You should be able to black the room out effectively so that after a few minutes with shutters closed on the window and a curtain over the door you cannot see any significant light leakage.

The enlarger needs a worktop like a small chest of drawers or a single kitchen base-unit, and most processors need a similar amount of space. You also need somewhere to put your box of paper and negatives, which should be near the enlarger (the 'dry' area) not the processor (the 'wet bench'). Everything should be at a convenient hand height as you have to work in darkness.

You need a power point for the enlarger and its electronic timer, and one for the processor, which usually incorporates a heater. We cannot go into the detail of printing here, but a visit to a major photo dealer will show you that enlargers vary greatly in price. The best idea is to start with a home colour darkroom kit. It will contain everything needed, with instructions, and when you no longer find it adequate there will always be someone else wanting to start printing their own.

Hire facilities

Our advice, however, is to hire a darkroom at a photographic centre. In Britain, excellent darkroom workshops exist in London, Cambridge, Southampton, Oxford, Derby and other towns and cities. Some are

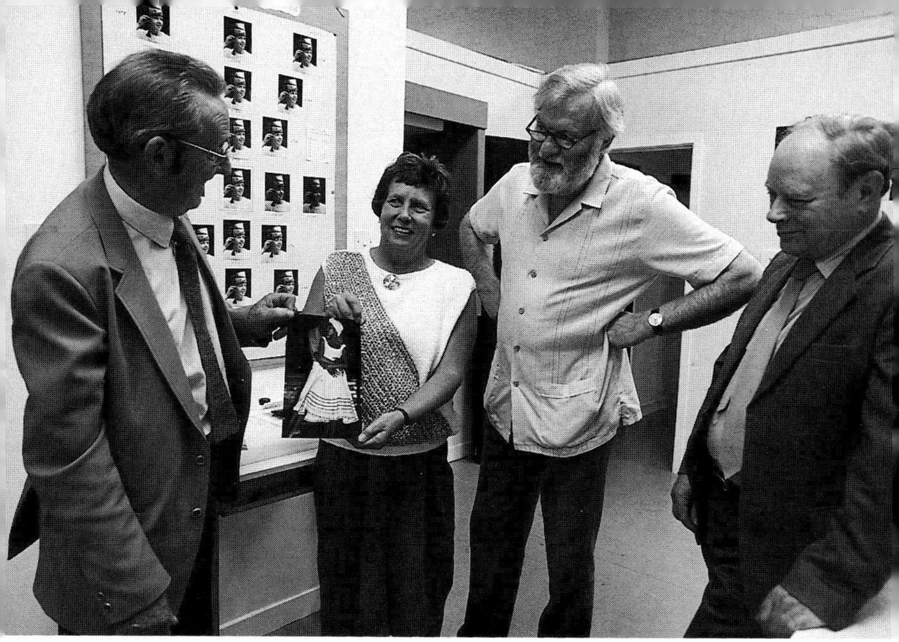

At John Cuerden's hire darkroom in Derbyshire holiday prints are discussed (top) before the photographer tackles colour enlarging

connected with colleges or galleries, others with manufacturers who sponsor them, and a few are privately owned. Many camera clubs also have their own darkrooms.

The cost of hire for a couple of hours is little more than the price of a roll of film, and some basic instruction is available free from the technician or lecturer in charge of the facilities. You may have to book in advance, but you will have none of the other commitments of darkroom work – if you decide you would like to try a 12 x 16" enlargement, the paper is there and available sheet by sheet. You would otherwise have to buy a pack of at least ten sheets to try it yourself.

Depending on the policy of the darkroom facility involved, the costs for a printing session may be very low. A typical price at the time of writing, with each sheet of 10 x 8" photographic paper costing £0.35, was £6.75 for three hours inclusive of chemicals.

A proficient user could make ten prints in this time, at a total cost which would only have purchased a single 10 x 8" hand-made print from a good colour laboratory (or three machine-made prints).

It is certainly worth taking your holiday photographs through this final stage, which is a good way to occupy a few afternoons in winter, and in the process you will learn a great deal about how and why photographs work – which will improve next year's holiday photographs too.

APPENDIX A: PROCESSING DATA

When on holiday you may buy unfamiliar makes of film. While it is always better to use a film you know, most modern films produce good results when processed correctly. The right processes for commonly-met films are listed below.

NEGATIVE colour film for making prints rather than slides
Process: **Kodak C-41** (Agfa AP-70, Fuji CN-16, Konica CNK-4)

Kodacolor VR100, 200, 400 and 1000
Kodacolor Gold 100, Gold 200, Gold 400
Ektacolor Gold
Vericolor III Type S, Vericolor HC, Type L
Fujicolor HR II 100, 200, 400, 1600
Konicolor SR100v, SR200, SR400, SR1600, SR3200
Agfacolor XRS100, XRS400, XRS1000

Nearly all other films ending in the term *-color* use this process including Forte, Tura, Oga, Negra, Perutz, Valca, 3M, Boots, Dixons, Revue, and Ilford but excluding some East German ORWO and Russian Techno films, which can only be processed in their country of origin. Ilford XP-1 black and white film can also be processed in C-41 chemicals. Colour negative films hardly ever include processing in the cost, and it is safe to buy any negative film with C-41 mentioned on the packaging for processing in Europe or the USA.
The C-41 process is the normal processing offered by one-hour and similar mini-labs.

REVERSAL colour film for making colour slides

Process: **Kodak K14** (Kodachrome)

Kodachrome 25, Kodachrome 64, Kodachrome 200
This process is unique to Kodachrome. The films can not be processed by ANY other process and no other films can be processed by Kodachrome laboratories. Amateur films sold in Britain and Europe include a process-paid mailer. Professional film or film sold in the USA and most other countries does NOT include processing.

Process: **Kodak E-6** (Agfa AP44, Fuji CR-56, Konica CRK-2)

Ektachrome 64, 100, 160, 200, 400, P800/1600*
Fujichrome 50, 64T, 100, 400, 1600
Konicachrome 100
Agfachrome RS50, RS100, RS200, RS1000

Nearly all other films with a name ending in *-chrome*, by makers as listed above by make, with the exception of East German ORWO. Many films are supplied for amateur use with process-paid mailers, which in the case of minor makes may only be usable in the country of origin; professional films are not supplied with mailers. You can use professional lab services to have a pre-paid film processed if the mailer is not valid in your home country, as long as the packaging mentions E-6 or a compatible process. *Special process E-6P is required for this professional Kodak film.

BLACK AND WHITE films can be processed anywhere in the world by conventional black and white methods. These vary greatly from place to place and results are rarely the same twice. Home processing in recommended.

APPENDIX B: EXPOSURE DATA

The exposures suggested here for major tourist attractions and typical subjects are based on data from the *Kodak Professional Data Guide,* a valuable pocket book for photographers which can be obtained from most photographic dealers.

EXPOSURES are given for film of MEDIUM SPEED ISO 100 for standard daylight conditions and popular holiday subjects. The exposures given for illuminations at night (etc) produce a result in which the lights are the main subject; do not expect the detail of the scene to be fully illuminated.

Bright or hazy sun on light sand or snow	1/250 s	*f*16
Bright or hazy sun (hard edged shadows), normal scene	1/250 s	*f*11
Bright or hazy sun, backlit or close-up subject	1/125 s	*f*8
Weak sun – soft shadows	1/125 s	*f*11
Cloudy Bright – no shadows	1/125 s	*f*8
Open Shade (shady area on a sunny day)	1/60 s	*f*8
Overcast – heavy cloud	1/60 s	*f*8
Skyline or seascape just after sunset	1/60 s	*f*4
Skyline or seascape 10 minutes after sunset	1/30 s	*f*4
Skyline – distant view of buildings with lit windows at night	4 s	*f*2.8
Shopping malls and brightly lit streets at night	1/30 s	*f*2
Shop windows	1/30 s	*f*2.8
Neon signs and other illuminated signs	1/30 s	*f*4
Floodlit buildings, fountains, monuments, Blackpool Tower (etc)	1 s	*f*4
Fairs, amusement parks, illuminations	1/15 s	*f*2
Moving traffic on motorways (light streaks)	20 s	*f*16
Moonlit snow scenes, full moon	15 s	*f*2
Moonlit landscapes, full moon	30 s	*f*2
Floodlit sports events, shows	1/30 s	*f*2
Spotlit acts, circuses etc	1/60 s	*f*2.8
Inside art galleries and museums	1/8 s	*f*2
Inside churches	1 s	*f*5.6
Christmas lights and tree lights, outdoors	1/30 s	*f*2

Stained glass windows from inside – 3 stops more exposure than outdoor conditions

INDEX

INDEX

ACKNOWLEDGMENTS

Photographs by:

A1 Studios: pages 9, 13, 14, 21, 40, 111, 112, 119, 120, 125, 127, 128, 129, 135

Richard Bradbury LMPA: Cover – child with melon; pages 117, 122

DIVER magazine/Eaton Publications: page 89

Derek Grossmark: 52, 92

David Kilpatrick AMPA: Cover – all other photographs; pages 11, 15, 19, 25, 27, 29, 30, 31, 35, 36, 37, 41, 44, 45, 46, 47, 49, 53, 54, 55, 56/7, 58, 59, 60, 61, 62, 65, 66, 67, 69, 75, 76, 77, 80, 82, 93, 101, 105, 108, 111 (bottom), 114, 116, 121, 124, 133

Shirley Kilpatrick: pages 23, 26, 68, 71, 85, 98/9, 113, 126

Duncan I. McEwan: pages 96, 104

Robert Motz: page 79

Minolta Club of Great Britain: pages 33, 87, 137

Janet Walkinshaw: page 100

Jerry Wooldridge FRPS: page 103 (courtesy Bronica UK Ltd)